"After reading this book, I recognize that today's most successful film directors and producers employ tactics similar to the Vector to achieve their stated goals. Taking a fleeting idea from one's imagination and willing it into a physical production attractive to a global market is an entrepreneurial achievement only visionaries and gravitators excel at. This book puts into writing what they practice—that every film production is a new start-up requiring its company to quickly mesh into a cohesive unit and all follow the same script. This is now recommended reading for my industry."

—Cabot McMullen, film & television producer

"We restructure companies with financial and strategic issues. Troubled companies oftentimes struggle with fatigued leadership and troubled employees. The Vector, if followed from an early stage in a company's life cycle, can keep the mission on track, saving hardship and the bottom line!"

—Dan Walsh, managing partner, BMP

"The Human Vector is a brilliant system for building highly efficient organizations. Oleg's approach combines science with the understanding of human behavior patterns so that it can accurately separate the wheat from the chaff in terms of employee productivity. It's a game changer for management's ability to build teams with members who can contribute to the longevity and prosperity of their organization."

—Marsha Friedman, founder, New

T0144834

"Kondrashov and Robertson have written an insightful analysis of the world labor market and its implications for the entrepreneurial organization. The Vector Concept is a unique construct based on Kondrashov's physics background, and it addresses one of the primary concerns of developing an organization to respond to, not just follow, the entrepreneur. In the initial phase of the company's trajectory, the recruitment and development of personnel, minimizing turnover and unproductive contributions, is the prime concern of the organization. Every entrepreneur out there can benefit from the processes in this book."

—**Jack Zubriski, consumer growth specialist**

"The Human Vector strikes a necessary chord with the Latin world, quite possibly solving the age-old problem of alignment. Across Central and South America and the Caribbean, a chasm exists between management and employees, mostly due to political and educational factors. These issues are reinforced by social and cultural norms, where the lines between work and socialization and friendship have become blurred, making it very difficult for management and HR to perform their functions. The Human Vector system solves this."

—**Stuart Robles, international growth specialist**

"This book has something for anyone interested in rapid change in business. Pandemic or no, companies need to move as one organism and adapt through technology. This book puts forth a methodology for the corporate pivot."

—**Amy Paxson, managing partner, Vox Marketing**

"Performance is vital to achieve our goals in business and personal life. With so many distractions, we can easily deviate from our goals, and the deviations lead us to different places than where we want to be, generating frustration and losing time and resources. The Human Vector fixes this. If applied correctly, it can even lead to a personal life of satisfaction in all areas, including love, career, family ... a life of fulfillment."

—Jose Muñoz, business coach, speaker, and CEO of ALLAGIS

"Bravo! At the heart of every successful organization, there are people with passion, drive, and an understanding of what defines success in their organization. The Human Vector provides a useful and systematic approach to maximizing employee results and productivity. All entrepreneurs building organizations from the ground up will find incredible takeaways from the teachings in this book."

—Amy Higgins, founder and CEO, Global Human Resources Group, people executive

"Robertson and Kondrashov have created a revolutionary model with The Human Vector. This is a vital missing component in our corporate workforce in this day and age. By scientifically defining the protocol and its application, they have created the optimal approach to maximize the potential of all employees in a corporation. Amazon, Apple, Google, and Tesla—take heed or be left behind!"

—Varun Choudhary, MD, MA, DFAPA, chief medical officer, Magellan Health

"As a founder of a behavioral health organization with five hundred employees, I found The Human Vector *fascinating and relevant reading. This systematic approach to all employees understanding and adopting the company culture will make for a much more harmonious workplace and save big money on onboarding the correct talent."*

—Matt Marek, founder and CEO, Good Neighbor

"I have had the good fortune of knowing Rod and Oleg for many years and have done business with both in multiple countries. Their blend of philosophy based on experience and new methodology has proven the Vector works."

—Henry Shterenberg, CEO, GTP Innovations Group

"The ability to quickly pivot during these troubled times has become a matter of survival during this pandemic. We as hedge fund managers were unprepared for the devastation of our operating businesses in our portfolio. The Human Vector *will become mandatory reading for our CEOs, as they will need to react quickly to future events in real time with all employees acting in unison."*

—Nameless hedge fund manager

"Corporate agility and adoption of new practices are a must to survive in the new world order postpandemic. Having the Vector as a guide to companies in growth mode before they get too big can set the foundation for success"

—Jim Sullivan, private equity investor

THE

HUMAN VECTOR

THE MAN FROM MINSK

PIVOT TO PROFITIBILITY

OLEG KONDRASHOV
ROD ROBERTSON

Published by Advantage, Charleston, South Carolina.
Member of Advantage Media Group.

ADVANTAGE is a registered trademark, and the Advantage colophon is a trademark of Advantage Media Group, Inc.

Printed in the United States of America.

10 9 8 7 6 5 4 3 2 1

ISBN: 978-1-64225-153-1
LCCN: 2020903546

Book design by Wesley Strickland.

This publication is designed to provide accurate and authoritative information in regard to the subject matter covered. It is sold with the understanding that the publisher is not engaged in rendering legal, accounting, or other professional services. If legal advice or other expert assistance is required, the services of a competent professional person should be sought.

Advantage Media Group is proud to be a part of the Tree Neutral® program. Tree Neutral offsets the number of trees consumed in the production and printing of this book by taking proactive steps such as planting trees in direct proportion to the number of trees used to print books. To learn more about Tree Neutral, please visit www.treeneutral.com.

Advantage Media Group is a publisher of business, self-improvement, and professional development books and online learning. We help entrepreneurs, business leaders, and professionals share their Stories, Passion, and Knowledge to help others Learn & Grow. Do you have a manuscript or book idea that you would like us to consider for publishing? Please visit advantagefamily.com or call 1.866.775.1696.

A unique new working environment built by EnCata that can be set up and dismantled in a short timeframe and at minimal cost.

CONTENTS

To learn more about the Vectors, supplemental software,
and other publications, visit www.kondrashov.biz.

PREFACE

The "Human Vector," as constructed and deployed by Oleg Kondrashov, our coauthor and "man from Minsk," has far-reaching consequences for organizations of all sizes. It is based on a scientific process and approach to organizational development to ensure maximum production by employees with minimum operational friction. We have all heard and read about Six Sigma and "lean" management ethics and related philosophies, but the VECTOR goes one step further in this evolution of forward-looking management.

In essence the Vector is a human pattern of behavior that analyzes and places individuals within the conformity of the organization's matrix. The Vector assists management in hiring the correct employees who conform to the organization's leadership and become an extension of ownership's will and strategic goals.

Oleg has developed an employee profile system that integrates work efforts, reduces stress in the workplace, and holds all employees and contractors accountable. The Vector system rewards great conduct and profitability with raises and perks. It also punishes employees with a reduction in pay and benefits, depending upon their contributions to the mother ship. As employees spiral away from the mantra of the organization, their access is restricted step by step, and they become isolated in many ways from their fellow workers. Either they get back on board, or they move to a graceful exit. There are no misunderstandings or rifts at employee termination, as all parties see a clear, regimented approach to their jobs that highlights both good and bad behavior.

Management can develop a systematic approach that makes all managers aware of the daily progress of each individual employee and deviations from the company's goals. This may sound rather heartless, but the Vector system certainly elevates employees' awareness of where they stand with management. With no place to hide or duck responsibilities, Vector-driven companies perform much better than their competitors. Management can actually manage from macro to micro as they deem fit, but they will always have the tools to make the correct call on employee performance as well as their own functions. Ownership and management will have no one to blame but themselves, as they will have a full array of data to make judgments on all levels of employees' performance.

FOREWORD

By Rod Robertson

In all my years of travel, adventure, and international intrigue, I have met a kaleidoscope of men and women that almost defies description. The uphill battle against repressive regimes, destitute countries, and third world issues we have all read about makes for serious obstacles in realizing one's dreams as an entrepreneur. Our new world postpandemic is bringing out the best and the worst in business leadership and ethics. The "old school" of reliance on doing face-to-face business is accelerating its way into the dustbin of history. New leadership from the tech-driven sectors will sculpt the future of world business.

My friend Oleg Kondrashov is one of the most fascinating men I have met. It is unusual for a man of thirty-five to write a business book, but his story should already be told. His exciting life of innovation and creating businesses from "ideas" will aid thousands in their quest for fame and fortune. Oleg goes beyond the hunt for wealth. His portfolio of companies has already deployed lifesaving products and technologies that will enhance many lives. He has led the proverbial "pivot" of his firms from companies paralyzed by the pandemic to firms producing a wide range of products that will assist in stemming the growth of the virus. He was able to adroitly switch gears mainly due to his "Vector theory," which we explore in this book.

The Vector premise, which has proven successful for Oleg and his team, has been greatly aided by the new world of business in 2020. Companies must evolve rapidly as one organism to meet new challenges. Adherence to the Vector will allow firms to shed traditional reactions to upheaval and make rapid decisions, ranging from strategic planning on the run to the evaluation of talent on board and the best use of their skill sets.

The pandemic has created opportunities for new business leaders to emerge on the world stage. The world's pivot in 2020 to "essential" (versus nonessential) businesses has seen a stampede of intellectual brilliance flare up around the world in humanity's quest for new science and tech advancements. Innovators such as Oleg will greatly enhance their countries' and the world's access to groundbreaking technology. The big companies will certainly dominate the headlines, but innovation often starts with ideas hatched in small circles around the globe.

Oleg has created an idea-processing machine, like the fabled Henry Ford did with his first assembly line. Oleg's operation has a "Funnel" that takes in the "best of the best" start-ups and companies that are ready to launch and need a methodology to their madness and go-to-market strategies. Oleg is a scientist who views the world of business differently than we Westerners do. Eastern Europe, having long lived under the shadow of the former Soviet Union, is still seeking its own rightful place in the world matrix of business and has tremendous dormant technology we all can monetize.

The former Soviet confederation spent enormous time, energy, and government focus on developing world-class technology in virtually all sectors. From this mammoth machine of the USSR, an educational system was built (and still thrives) that is equal to or surpasses the United States' development in certain sectors. Science and technology fields spawned from Eastern European educational institutions continue to deploy hundreds of thousands of world-class engineers, scientists, and computer-related programmers who need access to Western marketing and selling.

The majority of these Eastern European initiatives and projects are doomed to stagnate and die from lack of managerial foresight and funding. This fallow ground of world-changing technology should be harvested! This is what Oleg's and his team's life mission is. They are reaping the fields of bountiful technology and creativity and taking it to market in a systematic fashion.

As the world gets smaller and we use all the communication devices and banking sources at our disposal, bridges between European creativity and technology will mesh well with North America. Oleg and his team are on the cutting edge of this tsunami that will break upon the shores of America.

The costs of "offshore" Eastern European development are approximately 25 percent of comparable US services (i.e., salaries and full employment packages). The cost savings of offshore "back-office" skills that we Americans are somewhat aware of is the tip of the proverbial iceberg in future East-West synergies. Though each nation-state has set up physical borders for medical reasons and travel has greatly reduced, the use of technology is making business leaders cooperate as never before.

Oleg and his team have set a Funnel that churns out multitudes of great opportunities. He has developed a scientific machine to elevate the chances of success for these fascinating fledgling companies. I have not seen in all my years such an incubator as Oleg's, based on methodology that, like Henry Ford's assembly line, systematically takes a company from concept to launch in the global marketplace. At each step of the process, the subject firm in the incubator increases value, hammers management into reality, and elevates the product's performance. I have visited and participated at MIT and other renowned incubators and labs but have not found such a developed program with two hundred employees with higher-ed degrees like Oleg's.

The serious and curious reader alike should enjoy this book immensely. It is a marriage of East and West and best business practices; it elevates a company's chances for great success. It takes lean and Six Sigma practices to a new level that will be a guiding light for new, emerging technologies or rapid-growth organizations with global aspirations.

In a recent conversation I had with Oleg, he reflected in a way that I think sums it up beautifully: "Living in one of the most authoritarian countries in Europe, I oftentimes believe I can see our societies more clearly. My mission in life is much different than most others in Europe and America. Everything can be simplified here in my world. I don't need a weapon to make my country democratic. Innovations will be enough for that. Technoparks, new technologies, daily training—all that education will become a driver of democracy in Belarus. So do we really need to manufacture democracy by force? Maybe it's better to finally open an education center, not a military base."

DEFINITIONS AND TERMINOLOGY

THE VECTOR:

A systematic and scientific approach of management to assess, evaluate, and maximize employee performance.

GRAVITY:

The ability to attract other employees and change their Vector Angle.

VECTOR LENGTH:

The professionalism of an employee.

THE ANGLE:

Employees' loyalty to the organization and relationship to the Vector.

MATHLETE:

An individual with excellent mathematics skills.

THE GRAVITATOR:

An individual who is able to change Angles of employees by force of personality.

KPI:

Key performance indicator.

TRL:

Technology readiness level (developed by NASA).

INTEGRATION:

The movement and formation of Vectors; an incentive for growth.

INTEGRATOR:

A person who accelerates interactions between people in a company.

MASS EFFECT:

The process of mass interdependent chain changes in the Angles. Mass movement of employees can dilute or slow growth of the company Vector.

GRAVITATIONAL FIELDS:

Numbers of magnets (created by a company's ecosystem) that change Vectors of its employees.

FUNNEL OF VECTORS:

Acceptable deviation of employees from the company Vector.

DISINTEGRATOR:

A person who slows down or stops interaction between people in a company.

GENERAL VECTOR TIPS

1. The company founder is not just one example for the employees but also the main factor, determining the Vector of the business. Close interaction between the founder and the employee over a long period of time can lead to unpredictable consequences, burnout being one of them.

2. A specific management style must meet the company requirements at each stage of its growth. All founders should understand at what point it is best to offer the role of direct oversight to a more skilled manager in that area of operation.

3. Provide conditions for a favorable environment in your company, since this will contribute to the management of Vectors of the employed staff. Assess the feasibility of the employment of the established experts.

4. The interaction of employees' Vectors brings the system into equilibrium and produces a positive or negative common Vector of the team.

5. Mass unsystematic and thoughtless recruitment of employees to departments can lead to sad consequences—a negative impact on the atmosphere in the company—and reduce the effectiveness of the team down to failing business.

6. In order to form a more or less effective system, you need to divide employees according to certain parameters. In groups, you need to add employees with stable Vectors and gravity, as close as possible to the Vector of the company.

7. Gravity is the ability to attract other people. Identify Gravitators at the early stages, and work to get their loyalty. Implement strong and loyal Gravitators in the teams that require a change of the common Vector.

8. Imaginary Gravity is the informal Gravitator's impact on the team. Without a Gravitator, the work efficiency of the team will fall.

9. Quite often one of the employees, a supervisor, or a customer may be a Gravitator. A true Gravitator within the team is not always a leader.

10. A team can be built without any Integrator or Gravitator. Sooner or later a team player will emerge as a Gravitator or an Integrator.

11. Integrative management is impact on a person by Gravity to induce action.

12. The ability to change the Vector shows how much the employee is ready to take the influence of someone else's Gravity and Integration. The rate of Vector change depends on the type of activity, environment, and age of the employee.

13. The strong Vector effect comes from strong-minded entrepreneurs and allows them to create companies and manage a large business. Management and control over this effect are some of the fundamental tasks of a supervisor. During a business growth cycle, founders should withdraw and hand their duties over to a more suitable candidate or execute their decisions by

selecting outstanding employees resistant to the strong Vector effect, which is quite difficult at this stage.

14. Usually, the average intelligence level of a supervisor is higher than that of his or her subordinates. It is achieved if a supervisor stretches his or her mind and learns to make decisions under different circumstances.

15. The Gravitational Field of the company leads to the creation of a continuous stream of improvement of not only skills but also the moral qualities of the employee.

16. Tasks not related to work activity and successfully solved by the company maximize employee loyalty.

17. When you cease to engage in the development of corporate philosophy you remove the global Gravitational Field of the company. The longer the impact of a strong Vector and the general Gravitational Field is absent, the higher the probability of loss, not for individual employees, but for the company as a whole—the entire corporate system gradually collapses from the point of view of a general understanding of philosophy, starting with the most distant Vectors.

18. The process of continuous improvement is the basic principle of a modern company. It is necessary to track the development of each employee. Any stoppage in his or her development is regression and degradation. To ensure harmonious development, it is necessary to monitor and influence a number of factors that constantly affect the energy state of an employee.

19. The most important place in the system is prestage monitoring. It includes a survey and interview, monitoring and analysis of

the employee's behavior, conversation with the employee, and the study of the employee's productivity.

20. The system involves the subjective selection and combination of the methods on the basis of the collected and analyzed data during the prestages.

21. A Funnel of Vectors shows an acceptable deviation between the Vector of the candidate and that of the company on the basis of simple moral, ethical, and philosophical principles.

22. The creation of the Funnel is a goal of the HR manager individually. It is they who, over the course of multiple interviews, will compare the Vector of the candidate in relation to that of the company.

23. For the initial conversation and determination of whether the candidate fits in the Funnel or not, it is enough to compare your basic managerial moral norms and values with those of the potential employee.

24. Expression of excessive loyalty shouldn't always be taken as a signal to hire the candidate. It is important to differentiate loyalty from initial temporary chemistry, which will fade within the first month of working activity. As a result, the job seeker who seemed the most gung ho may end up being the wrong fit for the company.

25. A Gravitational Field is a number of magnets that attract prospective employees, change their Vectors, and hold the current colleagues in the correct position. When the Gravitational Field is "withdrawn," the system will go into the self-controlling mode and separate cultures of each division of the company will form.

26. For a successful and productive team, sector composition should not exceed seven to ten employees.

27. During the selection of the leader, it is necessary to follow the sequence of criteria for the formation of the leaders of the group: Gravity, Integration, loyalty, skills, property and the rate of change, and chemistry.

28. The total collective Vector is not only influenced by the founder of the Vector, but itself can also have a profound impact on the founder.

CHAPTER 1

BEYOND LEAN—A VOICE FROM THE EAST

Over the past few decades, the way people do business has changed dramatically. New technology and new management styles have shifted the needs and desires of the modern employee. Careers—once lifelong relationships between employee and company—are now constantly changing acquaintances. The pandemic has forever altered our workplace, where now technology and rapid pivoting is the new order of the day. The modern employee switches organizations at whim in order to get more money, better opportunities, and alluring benefits. At the same time, companies attempt to attract and retain top talent through higher salaries, overly competitive benefit structures, and company cultural restructuring. These contrasting forces have created a chaotic battleground where companies scramble to cater to the desires and impulses of employees. Meanwhile, employees are more than ready to ditch one opportunity for a better one.

Companies—American companies in particular—are doing very little to address this rising cultural tide. In fact, they actively support this hectic race. Their new and "innovative" human resources departments use precious marketing dollars to cultivate positive images in the media to attract fresh talent. They create new and fancy employment packages without considering how it will affect their bottom line. They offer incentives to the most talented employees without thinking how those employees will fit within their organization. While the rapid growth of technology means that we can do more with less, companies are continually being asked to give more to employees who are less engaged with the mission of the organization.

THE VECTOR IS A SYSTEMATIC AND SCIENTIFIC MANAGEMENT APPROACH DESIGNED TO MAXIMIZE EMPLOYEE PERFORMANCE AND ORGANIZATIONAL MOMENTUM. IN THE VECTOR APPROACH, THE FOUNDER SETS A CLEAR MISSION FOR THE COMPANY TO FOLLOW—THE VECTOR

Contemporary businesses need to understand that the elements of the labor market are in constant motion. Tracking the value of each candidate in relation to the company's moving target is impossible. The same difficulties arise in securing the best experts in the industry—companies with superior resources are outbidding each other for intellectual horsepower. All this scrambling is happening while companies must continue daily operations.

Companies must set goals that come from the founder. Only with a clear organizational mission can an employee see how they align with—or are distanced from—their organization's forward motion.

The pandemic fallout will see a delineation between companies that can morph quickly to meet demands and make painful cuts and those that can't. Each organization must now make hard decisions to change products, cut production, or hire and fire new employees at warp speed. But where should that mission come from? Who has the vision and leadership that can entice and unite people to achieve a common goal—a goal that is mutually beneficial for all parties involved and that creates a sense of pride and motivation? It's clear an organization's goals—to serve clients and gain profit—are often at odds with those of their employees. Only the founder of a company can bring those two opposing perspectives into balance. The company should set goals that should come from the founder and create goals where a financial reward is only a piece of the motivation. With a clear mission from the founder, the chaos of the pull of employees and the push of an organization can be brought into balance, and based on this mission, the organization's **Vector** can be found.

The **Vector** is a systematic and scientific management approach designed to maximize employee performance and organizational momentum. In the Vector approach, the founder sets a clear mission for the company to follow—the Vector. The founder then finds **Gravitators**—employees who believe in the mission of the founder. **Gravitators** also can change the mission of other new employees in order to rally them behind the founder. These Gravitators become the building blocks of teams. They also keep themselves attuned to the Vector so that they can best lead their teams in accomplishing that mission. Finally, the Vector is used to create **key performance indicators** that allow management to accurately assess the value of an employee. The Vector ensures balance between the needs and wants of the employee and the operations and maintenance of the company.

There are many ways to achieve this balancing act of the Vector in a company. By reading this book, you are taking the first steps of a long journey toward that balance. At my firm, it was a long discovery process, but in the end we created a company that aspires to this balance. We did so by adopting best practices from both Eastern and Western schools of thought.

In the Eastern European work model, an employee can easily

adhere to high standards in his or her work. Therefore, at the start, EnCata did not create any meaningless corporate culture. It's not normal for a company to do this. In fact, it was hard work. But we felt that it would drastically reduce bullying, harassment, and discrimination. We also believed it would avoid empty gestures from the company to the employee. On the whole, our philosophy excludes these actions. At EnCata, we want our employees to have a personality match. We want them to believe in the company as much as the company believes in them. We fall short and make mistakes, of course, but we are constantly striving for balance.

For the last ten years, my team has synthesized and experimented with business and HR processes in order to rewrite an old story of corporate philosophy. Ours is not always a story of success. It was through realizing the mistakes that could be corrected that brought us to fascinating new results. In this book each and every miscalculation will be accompanied by true examples. The entire history of our company will be laid bare for you to learn from. We hope our failures can be your successes in running an organization.

We are an ecosystem supported by the life events of my colleagues. Throughout this process, we've shared many memories, which I am now happy to share with you. I am not a primary source of knowledge about business and hiring, but I believe my message will resonate with you. This work will not be a fundamental study of human nature, but I will present every instance of our philosophy with facts that support our case. Lastly, I will make sure that after reading this book, you will not be left with just words but with the building blocks of your own philosophy toward creating a more balanced organization.

This book is a manual for any business owner who seeks to take his or her organization into the next generation of hiring and employee management. It is a brief guide to structuring a new hiring process that ensures all needs are being met. At the heart is the Vector and its value. The Vector allows organizations to understand the difference or similarity between the mission of the founder and the mission of a potential employee. This value, while not always as accurate as mathematics, allows hiring managers to make honest evaluations of potential new employees. It also gives managers accurate tools to maximize performance for these individuals.

Throughout this book, we will constantly turn to physics—the science that became the pillar of my education. The Vector approach brings a much-needed balancing force to our current chaotic work environment. We will use physics as a way to illustrate and symbolize this search for balance. In this way, we hope that science can open a new door of understanding for the world of high-tech business.

AT THE HEART IS THE VECTOR AND ITS VALUE. THE VECTOR ALLOWS ORGANIZATIONS TO UNDERSTAND THE DIFFERENCE OR SIMILARITY BETWEEN THE MISSION OF THE FOUNDER AND THE MISSION OF A POTENTIAL EMPLOYEE

However, it is not just the founder who has a mission. In fact, each and every one of us has to calculate our own Vector. Whether you are at the entry level or in the inner circle, your mission is invaluable to the forward momentum of your career. It is the employee's Vector, the company's Vector, and their correlation that becomes the foundation of a harmony within the team and employee development.

At EnCata, we learned this lesson the hard way. Many of the individuals on our team have worked through both the most recent economic recession and the collapse of the Soviet Union. By lasting through these tumultuous times, we've become battle hardened.

Our shared experience helped create a unique business culture that thrives despite outside adversity. Now, our company is a multifaceted organization with over fifty business units serving clients around Eastern Europe.

Our company is headquartered in Minsk, Belarus. Western readers might better know Belarus from our association with the Soviet Union. Your high school history teachers might have painted a different picture of our country. Hidden from the civilized world deep behind the Iron Curtain, Belarus was part of the "Evil Empire" of the USSR. The clichés, however, might be truer than you think. Starting any business in a country where entrepreneurial business was considered a crime is difficult. We spent the better part of a century operating under Soviet authority. Despite this, however, we created a company with unique HR practices that we now wish to share with you.

Throughout the USSR, citizens were forced to think that business embodied self-interest and individualism. That was the way to justify Communist ideology and its main principle—everyone should give away what they can and take whatever is necessary. The ideas of Communism were noble and intended for a very good cause. But in the end, this way of thinking led to the demise of the Soviet Union. These ideals of doing the best for your fellow man contrasted with the reality of living in the Soviet Union. For decades, we comrades in the USSR were proud of having more nuclear missiles while standing in a mile-long queue for bread. And even then, we were being asked to sacrifice more and more by our fearless leaders. We knew that something was very wrong.

Our state-planned economy simply could not fight the shortage of consumer goods. Our government drove its best and brightest deep into the military industrial complex, which did not feed back into the economy. During this economic death spiral in the USSR, any slight initiatives by workers to create innovation in the private sector were severely punished by the state. Those who dared to bring goods from behind the Curtain and sell them on the gray market were handed serious sentences. Commerce was crushed in the bud. Entrepreneurs were misunderstood and branded hoodlums.

The gradual crumbling of the Soviet Union left a mark with each country of the former USSR. And some of these countries are still dealing with the ramifications. While the Iron Curtain was demolished over thirty years ago, its foundational ideas remain unshakable in the minds of its citizens. The generation that now governs post-Soviet countries can still be antagonistic toward business development. While they support entrepreneurs and innovative business solutions, it is often to collect taxes on these growing businesses. The retiring generation struggles to understand the main point of innovations. They were not trained for this. At the same time, some authorities still see businesspeople as enemies from whom something needs to be snatched. This horrid practice of the past still dogs us innovators in the former Soviet bloc.

SYNTHESIZING THE BEST PRACTICES OF THE WEST AND SOVIET IDEALS WAS HOW WE CREATED THE VECTOR SYSTEM.

Many employees in the post-Soviet countries believe that their leaders earn cosmic profits solely thanks to the efforts of their subordinates. This is most likely due to the reputation that businesspeople have in our former Soviet bloc country. My generation, however, is just beginning to influence popular opinion, and people's attitudes toward business and innovation are gradually changing. Belarusians can start this change by taking on the best from the experience of Western countries and using that to forge our own path to success. This path will be hard and long, the path that we have to take together. But synthesizing the best practices of the West and Soviet ideals was how we created the Vector system.

Most former Soviet countries have taken different roads. Estonia, Lithuania, and Latvia became members of the European community as early as 2004. Ukraine has lately been struggling to become a part of the European Union. Central Asian countries have retained their relationship with Russia. It is only Belarus that has not chosen its path—a country with amazing engineering potential and a unique geographical location, and the country that gave life and education to the author of this book. My home country still remains a mystery to the Western world.

In case you forgot where Belarus is, it lies to the east of Poland and west of Russia. It is an independent country with the most unemotional people on the planet. We rarely smile at each other. We have few sunny days, and we are not very friendly at first sight. But at the same time, we are always ready to help a stranger, ready to open our doors to those who need it.

Yes, we share similarities with the Russian lifestyle, but geographically and mentally, we have always been closer to Europe. Nevertheless, many wars tormented our country over the last century. But we don't mourn those tragedies. Today we are proud of our experience and of what we have that has made us. We're a country of highly educated workers eager to get the job done. We have incredible engineering potential from dormant Soviet technologies. Lastly, we're able to do things at a fraction of the cost of our Western friends.

In the times of the Soviet Union, Belarus was an assembly shop for the huge superpower. We received accessory parts from the Far East, Baltic states, and Kazakhstan, which we then turned into tractors, buses, dump trucks—an endless variety of machines. We assembled whatever needed to be assembled. These powerful manufacturing capabilities were carefully passed on to the present generation of Belarusian engineers. We are excellent crafters who still undervalue our worth.

In the USSR there was no selling of any products in the country; all material resources were distributed centrally in accordance with our strict economic plan. Industrial enterprises hardly had time to bridge any deficit; there was no accounting or profit and loss. When we faced capitalism, it was the sales processes that caused bewilderment. All of a sudden, we realized we were unaware of the potential of business. We always made great products, but once the things were made and shipped, our job was done. The Belarusians never needed to market our products.

After almost thirty years of freedom, we are still learning how to sell ourselves to the West. We position ourselves as a higher-priced outsourcing option compared to other countries such as Ukraine and India. Our Western partners have considerable experience in this kind of outsourcing. It was the Belarusian state that acted as a guarantor and assistant in creating engineering services exports.

In Minsk, the capital of Belarus, High-Tech Park (HTP) was founded, perhaps the most successful project implemented across the country. This project brought together many companies engaged in the development of software for foreign customers via the outsourcing model. HTP exports software development services in excess of $2 billion every year and is annually growing by 10 percent. But this is only the beginning. The figure cited above is only a small percentage of our potential; it represents just the export of our software services. With our legions of educated engineers and programmers, Belarus has the capacity to increase the export of engineering services.

Under such conditions five years ago, a company called EnCata was created—an engineering catalyst and innovative service that embodies the most challenging ideas of our time. It took us years to hire the best specialists in Belarus. It's those brilliant individuals who inspire me to share the team-building experience in the pages of this book. It's those friends and partners who helped create the Vector philosophy I share with you now.

CHAPTER 2

WHY THE HUMAN VECTOR?

As we're all aware, the world is getting smaller every day. Business, on the other hand, is growing at an exponential rate. Now more than ever, many business decisions must be made almost simultaneously as companies fight for survival. Employees will also be engaged with ownership and embrace the Vector, as survival is at stake. These times have created the perfect ingredients for cohesive decision-making and implementation of strategies. In every economic crisis, rapid response is mandatory for future employment. Before, job hopping was an option. Now, however, with bleak opportunities, it is best for workers to contribute maximum performance, as the alternatives are grim. And new businesses are being discovered and founded every day. Business is a racetrack to get bigger and faster at any cost; those who fall behind are forgotten within weeks. Profitability is often sublimated by the drive for corporate "footprints" worldwide. With the dissolution of traditional country borders, it is literally a land grab out there. Work-forces are becoming populated by a more diverse set of ethnicities as we move to a truly integrated global economy.

With America's multicultural employment base, there are many stress points and drags on efficient business practices. Unlike homogenous societies operated by folks of the same culture, America truly is a stew of different perspectives that sometimes make it hard for us to connect over a common mission. The Human Vector, as developed by Oleg and his team, should be welcomed by American corporations that are seeking to expand and become more efficient. The Vector can fuse a company together, having employees and management work as one team. This harmony will create more productivity overall.

America needs the Human Vector strategies more than ever! A diverse cultural workforce like that of the United States demands a set of hypersensitive HR guidelines that ensure all hired employees align to the company's Vector. Nowadays, mission-minded employees are a luxury for hiring managers. The Vector makes them an unquestionable need. The money spent on onboarding employees now compiled with the complexities of termination make selection and integration paramount. Virtually all tech companies are in a race against time.

As companies race to market with growth strategies, they cannot be hobbled with constant turnover, internal disputes, or corporate malaise. In a Vector-aligned business, such interpersonal disputes would be alleviated. Employees would understand that these sensitivities are obstacles to achieving the company goals. This book is not written to judge what is appropriate for the working environment. Rather, it is to ensure that all employees are pulling together with minimum discord.

In prepandemic times, remote work was for 10 percent of the workforce, and it was viewed suspiciously by management. Now, however, the pendulum has swung the other way. Soon a new normal will set in that, according to experts, will have 30–40 percent of the workforce working remotely. These remote employees must be fully committed to the company and not just be working for a day's pay. It's rather easy now to have everyone's attention during a crisis, but when the dust settles and the new reality emerges, then the Vector will truly be needed.

The coronavirus outbreak, which at the time of this writing has infected millions and is growing exponentially, is another reason why the Vector is so important for the world workplace. Having unsupervised employees working independently can be risky for multiple reasons. The Vector would ensure you have hired the right people that believe in the company mantra and will perform their task no matter the locale. Until recently most organizations were reluctant to have offsite workers, but now there has been a huge shift to allowing workers to telecommute and protect those in the office from communicable diseases. With this shift, adherence to the company Vector is a must.

So many growth-oriented companies—ranging from giants like Google to the newest start-ups—evangelize harmony in the workplace. These "Kumbaya" moments have the millennial population drinking the company Kool-Aid by the gallons (or in-office beer kegs). However, a culture without a mission can't create that harmony. The Vector system can make sure the right human ingredients are present to make the Kool-Aid more than just a sugary, empty promise.

IN ORDER TO STAY COMPETITIVE, AMERICA MUST EMBRACE NEW TECHNOLOGY AND BUSINESS METHODOLOGIES FROM EUROPE AND ASIA.

Is America listening to the call coming from around the globe? Is this the time for America to pull back on American trade and right the wrongs of cumulative generations? Is America ready to become an outsider in the world business community? Already, America is beginning to pull back its holdings—both economically and militarily—across the world. In this withdrawal, a vacuum is being created. And Asia is rushing to fill the void left behind. China and the Asian powerhouses such as Singapore are gathering momentum to shift global economics in Asian favor.

With the paralyzing issue of coronavirus, the distinct trend of China and Asian power rising to world prominence as an economic force has received a sucker punch. What was seen as a foregone conclusion of Asian proliferation has now ground to a halt and may never recover. It remains to be seen whether Asian power will wane with the world economy shuddering in 2020.

In order to stay competitive, America must embrace new technology and business methodologies from Europe and Asia. Western Europe has already awakened to the growing titans of the East and is rapidly disengaging from the United States to seek new alliances with Asian powers. Russian trade with China alone is close to $100 billion and rapidly growing. With the completion of the Belt Road Initiative (BRI) funded by China, new superhighways will cut across Asia to Europe, connecting four billion folks from different cultures. This mammoth Eurasian project all but ensures greater business alliances between Western Europe and Asia.

Before the pandemic, European and Asian trade was reaching $2.5 trillion—double European-American business. And this gap continues to grow. Europe not only needs products and financing from Asian countries; it needs workers as well. The birth rate replacement in any country is 2.1 people per family, which will allow a country to maintain a stable population. European birth replacement rates are aggregating at approximately 1.4 per household, while Asia is propagating at upward of 3.0. Europe needs Asian workers, and they are rapidly shifting their policies to everyone from Philippine workers to Indian tech leaders.

Each country must look to develop its current workforce. The United States went from virtually zero tech unemployment to total chaos, with a third of the workforce unemployed. The resiliency of America will allow these employees to be reintegrated, but with far-reaching consequences. They will come back under terms and conditions that they elevate their game and must once again prove their worth to the company very rapidly. Balance sheets and financial forecasts will dictate employment as never before, as companies will not have the reserves (or customers) to warrant big R&D cycles. Strategies and profits will be tied very closely together.

Though the world has radically changed, it is still of interest to put events of the past into perspective. Eastern Europe, Russia, and the former countries of the Soviet Union are all looking east to these new powers. They realize, however, that they can offer America a huge stopgap in the economic brain drain to Asia. Russia, since the 1940s, has developed fantastic educational systems that were the world's counterpart to America, as both countries fought for supremacy for five decades. The former Soviet Union spent a disproportionate amount of its gross national product (GNP) on heavy industry related to the military and related sciences. In the end, this overexpenditure on nonconsumer products was a leading factor in the dissolution of the Soviet Empire. That being said, the reason for its downfall has been a boon for many of the former Soviet states.

Both Belarus and Ukraine have been massive industrial complexes and manufacturing countries. They were big parts of the engine of the Soviet Union and greatly benefited from the institutions that graduated millions of highly educated scientists and engineers. And the education hasn't changed since they gained their independence from Russia. In fact, it has even flourished.

Belarus in particular has been viewed by Europe and its former overseers in Moscow as a true technologically advanced country with huge human capital operating in hardware and software industries. Belarus—with a population of nine million—offers the best of the former Soviet Union's educational systems, which have been upgraded over the years. Belarus remains friendly with its neighbor Russia yet continues to export its bounty of scientists, programmers, and engineers to the United States and Europe. These highly educated Belarusian professionals lead a humble life. Their standard of living is low compared to that of the West, and their wages are about half those of their American counterparts.

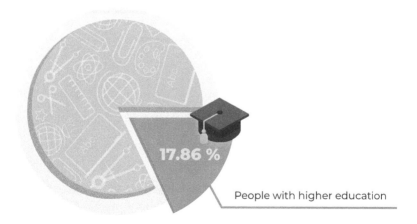

17.86 %

People with higher education

The current economic contraction has made this workforce more diligent than ever. Virtually all employees are eager to adhere to their leader's Vector or face the consequences of bleak employment if terminated. Nothing like hard times to get everyone's attention!

The massive retraction of the world economy is having consequences beyond anything any of us could have foreseen. The educational systems will churn out a new generation of employees without jobs, and companies will be cautious in hiring employees that will not directly impact profitability. As an example, life science companies in the States usually have a huge lead time for their products to go to market. This luxury has changed overnight. Firms that have not been approved by the FDA and are not near a product breakthrough will lead to the abandonment of many promising and much-needed products. Speculation is that there could be up to a 40 percent cut in life science budgets.

The new world suspicion of a Chinese cover-up of the origins of the pandemic and its related fallout many believe will unhorse China's rise to dominance. The mounting resentment of the fallout of the pandemic will make for seismic shifts in the country's relationships. Already there is a call for America to bring back essential manufacturing with the understanding that consumer prices will rise. This increase in the cost of consumer goods and anticipated inflation caused by the pandemic will have countries resolute in becoming as self-sufficient as possible.

But no matter this internalized retrenchment of import and export, there will always be a need for cost-effective, highly trained technical people. Especially in our new age of technology that we must all embrace.

A natural sequence is now unfolding in American firms seeking Eastern European offshore tech services. Here is an example:

A New York–based advertising and digital agency has rapidly grown to $100 million in sales due to its "offshoring" of its programmers and coders to Ukraine. With over eighty tech employees in Eastern Europe, the firm pays annual salaries of $30,000 for in-line scientists and other key employees. In the States the firm was having to pay upward of $200,000 in packages with ridiculous benefits. Their employees were constantly poached, and recruiter fees were outrageous. The firm could not grow, as maintaining talent through their growth cycle was daunting. With a bold move to Eastern Europe, the firm saved approximately $6 million in annual salary and related expenses. This, translated at a multiple of seven times the EBITDA valuation, increased the value of the company by approximately $40 million. The firm now has a reservoir of talented high-end professionals in Europe that will smoothly fuel further expansion.

Belarus and its capital, Minsk, have a key role to play for US and Western European firms that are seeking a steady flow of quality work in R&D, software, and hardware development. Quality and experienced professionals combined with vastly reduced pricing and the ability to scale up and down make great options for US tech companies.

The United States always has been and will always be a chaotic hodge-podge of conflicting cultures driven by the ambitions of its individuals. The divisions and the cracks are becoming clear even to its citizens. The talking heads, slanted media, and constant political clashing has torn huge holes in the American fabric. The public is painfully aware now that the political system has become so polarized that there will be no turning back to the respect garnered by former presidents.

America is now a land of clashing cultures. The constant inflow of immigrants has kept our population at an excellent level of growth (2.2 birth replacement rate) that ensures a flow of new workers. Much of this growth, however, is taking on the manual or blue-collar positions. Any foreign thought leaders we once had are now returning home as their homelands become more palatable to reside in. The influx of Asian citizens has been a boon to all levels of American society. Currently there are twenty million Asians in America, of which five million are Chinese, four million are Indian, four million Filipino, and two million Vietnamese and Korean. Of the total population of California, 16 percent is Asian, and that statistic is growing rapidly.

The demographic diversification of America is accelerating. It is projected that in the next fifty years, minorities will grow to majorities. America's multiple cultures make for enormous stress and friction in the workplace. Language barriers, cultural diversities, and differing work ethics make for tense hiring and integration processes at work. It is no surprise that there is more stress and misunderstanding in America's workplace than anywhere else in the world.

America's economic foes work as a team in harmony within their country and their economic zone. Scandinavians and other homogeneous societies all have the same cultural DNA. They press ahead as a team in an ecosystem that puts them at the highest standard of living. There is no constant turmoil; they view the world from the same prism. As in the case of China, government backs business. The whole socioeconomic infrastructure of Chinese society is pulling together to seek economic dominance. Here is an example:

The world bicycle market is rapidly evolving. First the Europeans led the market, followed by the Americans, but now the Chinese have decided to take over this marketplace. The Chinese government has subsidized the cost of manufacturing by up to 50 percent of the cost of goods and has crushed most every competitive manufacturer. The combination of state and commerce working together trumps all normal business ventures.

American corporations are bogged down by cultural and HR issues that do not plague those in other countries. As an example, Victoria Robertson of the firm Fuze has recently cited the discrepancy between male and female wage earners. Compared to men, female ethnic groups receive the following percentages of men's executive compensation:

Asian women receive 86 percent of men's compensation.
White women receive 78 percent of men's compensation.
Black women receive 66 percent of men's compensation.
Latino women receive 58 percent of men's compensation.

This disparity obviously leads to much turmoil and resentment in organizations, which creates drag and stress on companies as they seek to grow. American firms are handicapped in the world arena by many cultural issues that just don't exist for their international competitors. The United States needs to adopt practices to level the playing field—and thus, we introduce the development of the Vector philosophy.

As each country has raised physical barriers and citizens stay at home, many experts say this could be the new norm. Virus hot spots and future flare-ups, as well as fear of travel and being caught abroad, are deep concerns that override career aspirations. The "stay at home" and social distancing orders could pertain to nation states. Hopefully racial and social barriers and prejudices will be lessened as corporations and countries see self-preservation of their way of life.

The Human Vector is more important than ever for firms to overcome racial and social norms from prepandemic days. Countries and corporations must cohesively follow leadership in their quest for creating the best living and working environment for all of us. There is no doubt the world is heading into a bleak short-term future, but we should adhere to teamwork, team building, and united work efforts to bring our standard of living back to prepandemic days.

CHAPTER 3

THE MAN
FROM MINSK

I was born into a tumultuous time when rapid political changes over-whelmed my home country of Belarus. This time of transitioning regimes resulted in a feeling of uncertainty throughout Eastern Europe. Despite the geopolitical chaos, however, my father did his best to make my childhood amazing and full of adventure. He was a colonel in the Soviet military and the head of a tank regiment deployed in East Germany (DDR). He was a man of iron will, the kind of man who symbolized the strength and power of the former Soviet Union. He was a man of integrity and morals. However, the fall of the Soviet Union surprised him.

There was hardly a dull moment throughout my childhood. When I was only a year old, my father realized that I had been stricken with a fatal disease and was close to death. Knowing he only had days to save my life, he commandeered a regimental helicopter and flew me to

Minsk, the capital of Belarus. I was saved at the last moment. His superiors were furious that he would fly off with a helicopter while a whole regiment of attack helicopters was on war footing. They came to understand, however, the seriousness of the situation. He survived that incident, but the fall of the Soviet Union created even more remarkable adventures for our family.

Another daring adventure from my life occurred while we were living in Berlin, Germany. I was six at the time, and the area was tense with conflict. The Berlin Wall was coming down, and Soviet personnel were suddenly targets for enraged Germans. Ugly confrontations between Germans and Soviets unfolded all throughout the city. The fighting became so bad that it eventually led to a mass evacuation of Russian military personnel and their families. My family was no different and was asked to begin evacuation procedures.

My father, as a commanding officer, had a military jeep and a driver. As I vividly recall, our car was surrounded by rioting Berliners bent on flipping over our vehicle. An angry crowd of skinheads and other rioters were violently rocking our car. My family and I were getting ready for the worst when my father took action. He jumped on top of the jeep and lifted a machine gun into the air, emptying a clip of ammo into the sky. The thugs scattered, and my father stood tall that day for his country and his family.

My father was strong and resolute in his values. As the Soviet Union began to crumble, many military officers turned to pillaging and profiteering as chaos consumed the military. My father, however, did no such thing. He stood on his principles and looked on these men with disdain. To him, they had become vultures who sold not only their tanks, but their dignity.

In my eyes, my father was a first-rate **Gravitator** and taught me the power of the Vector early on. His regiment was his company, and he was its leader. He placed excellent **Integrators** around him who amplified his unique and fluid style of command. His discipline, however, didn't stop me from having a troubled childhood.

Until the fifth grade, I was lazy and unmotivated but had an immense love for mathematics. In a sense, my malaise was a reflection of the realities of our withering society. Perestroika was a confusing time for us, where our actions felt meaningless. With each cascade of new political events, we felt we were catapulting out of control. To add insult to injury, each month we became poorer and poorer.

Our huge country was gradually moving toward defeat in the Cold War. Life had long ceased to be like the one that the Soviet campaign posters promised. The bright future had already darkened, so studying hard in my ordinary Minsk school felt futile. I had ominous thoughts for one so young. In these formative first years of my life, I learned how collective thinking can affect a person—even a small, disorderly child such as myself. Due to the need for a collective spirit, I was not steered away from the bad company in the schoolyard. Eventually, I became its leader. It was not a children's game but rather a group of malcontents that gathered around me.

It was my parents who eventually yanked me out of the gloomy clouds of my malaise and angst. They instinctively knew that I was a

Mathlete and worked with me to develop my math skills. They had me sit for rigorous math exams, which I passed with flying colors. I eventually found myself in new gifted math classes. To my own surprise, the dynamic was completely different than in my primary school. With my primary school colleagues, if a student tried to learn, they were laughed at. In these new classes, it turned out to be quite

the opposite. Good students were seen as cherished members of the class.

At first, I found myself a complete failure. Joining the class was like jumping onto a moving train. While I was slow at first, my mind began to grasp the concepts being taught to me. I made quantum leaps in theory and eventually caught up with my classmates. I even outshone a few of them by getting high final scores. Soon, I entered the prestigious BSU Lyceum. After that, I attended the leading Belarusian State University, where I started learning the basics of physics.

At this time, I was not even eighteen and had already changed my life. I was looking forward to a career as a scientist or engineer. I would have been more than happy with either of these prospects. My life, however, would turn out differently. A few days before my eighteenth birthday, my father passed away. Suddenly, I had become the provider for my family.

My first business was refilling printer cartridges. It was simple and profitable—at least it seemed that way at first. As a first-time business owner, I found it easy to deal with the technical parts of the business, whereas I had trouble managing my employees. I have always tried to run an "open books" system with my employees: I gave each one of them free access to the company's accounts. I sincerely believed that it would motivate my fellow coworkers to work better and bring profitability to the company. I believed that if an employee had

MY FIRST EMPLOYEES WERE DRIVEN BY CASH ONLY. AND WHEN HARD TIMES HIT, THEY HIT THE ROAD.

stakes in the company, they'd earnestly want it to succeed. But the overall horrendous economic situation kept my employees from thinking about anyone but themselves. My first employees were driven by cash only. And when hard times hit, they hit the road. After that moment, my "all for one and one for all" management style went out the window. I learned a very hard lesson on the reality of cash flow and loyalty—or the lack thereof.

During these trying times, I was combining work and university studies. Being the CEO of a new Belarusian company seemed like a far-off dream. Over the next ten years, I studied and redefined the Toyota production system and lean production. I experimented with TRIZ and Adizes techniques to create a unique corporate philosophy. In all these instances, I gleaned experiences that helped me tinker and create the business model known as the Vector. The only thing left to do was to try it out in the real world. I founded EnCata to implement my Vector philosophies. Now EnCata is an international company with offices in Belarus, the United States, the Czech Republic, Russia, Belgium, and Oman.

We focus on working with engineers and engineering products. We initiate product start-ups. We invest and help put the most daring engineering ideas in motion. Each office has a specialty, depending on the region in which it is located. These can be sales offices, development centers, or the R&D center—the heart of our operations. R&D centers carry out engineering development and product prototyping. These centers are based on workflow principles and minimize the losses that usually occur when transferring people, products, and information from one site to another. By reinvesting our profits in the equipment inventory and engineering personnel, we hope to become an even more prominent player in the global market of innovations.

THE SPECIFICS OF THE VECTOR PHILOSOPHY REQUIRE THE SEARCH FOR PROFESSIONALS, PEOPLE WILLING TO WORK IN A SPIRIT OF THE COMPANY.

Also under the leadership of EnCata, we have opened the "MakeIT Center," a "fab lab" where engineers and students can use the most modern equipment for research and prototyping. The MakeIT Center showcases how EnCata's journey has been one of self-education. We've pushed ourselves to grow and develop our own structure that challenges the status quo. This structure embraces an employee's identity and supports it by finding their own Vector and how it can fit within the company's Vector of development.

It is obvious that any recruitment agency will help you assess the skills of an employee. But only you are able to assess their loyalty and potential effectiveness. The specifics of the Vector philosophy require the search for professionals, people willing to work in a spirit of the company. That is why, at EnCata, all personnel solutions are made by me, our HR partner, and the heads of the departments.

A company should possess the same qualities as its leadership team at each stage of development. EnCata's philosophy of working with each start-up is based on a systematic growth and implementation with strategic thinking in a specific industry for further business development. Each project for us is a child that we carefully nurture, protecting it from unnecessary disturbances. Each employee is a spouse or kinsperson for the company, carefully selected and supporting the company even in difficult times. The HR department that uses the Vector theory is like the parent who approved the choice. Having spent my life's work developing EnCata, it has become my go-to method for making decisions.

CHAPTER 4

VECTOR POWER

Every person is fated to see the world through their own eyes. For many of us, these perspectives are shaped by the professions, positions, and passions we choose. Photographers view life through a camera. Prisoners see it through bars, and policemen, down the barrel of a gun. To them, every toy gun is a new threat. Think for a moment how your own career path has shaped your perspective.

Let's look at how prison guards are shaped by their work. These individuals spend all their professional lives surrounded by "involuntary guests" whom they treat as their wards. The culture of the prisoners, however, influences these guards more than they might think. In fact, I'd bet if you stripped them of their uniforms, they'd be indistinguishable from their "guests" in the penal system.

Remove these guards from the system, set them to a new task, and you will see a radical change. As humans, we are always affected by each individual who comes into our lives. Furthermore, our Vectors bend and change to adapt to the Vectors of those surrounding us. These changes and fluctuations cannot be determined with figures alone.

In fact, companies also go through changes—just as an individual does. It's almost impossible to predict how these transformations will affect their relationship to the labor market. A highly skilled new recruit might be unaffordable for a company at one point, but they might have the opportunity to hire them in the future. It's almost as if the employee is on one train, running parallel to a train that the company is driving. It would be very difficult for the employee to make the jump while the train is moving or for the company to extend a helping hand. These moving targets are incredibly difficult to hit. That is why we have developed an "employment system" that helps the company aim for these employees before we pull the trigger on hiring.

This system is based on the biggest needs of the employer and the employee's current Vector. We then distill that into a value that can be measured. By examining how a potential new employee can either add or detract from that value, we can make an informed hiring decision. This value allows us to assess the company's expectations and how the employee meets them.

THE KEY TO SUCCESS IS MATCHING THE EMPLOYEE'S MULTITUDE OF FORCES WITH THAT OF THE ORGANIZATION.

It can also be used to inform how the HR department will manage that employee and ensure they are moving the company forward. Every employee has a role in attaining the company's goal and mission.

A Vector, in mathematics, is characterized by its length and direction. In physics, we use many of these Vectors in common equations. You might know these Vectors by their more common names—force, speed, acceleration, torque, and so forth. Just as these forces exist in the natural world, so, too, do they exist in the world of business. And the key to success is matching the employee's multitude of forces with that of the organization.

It is the Vector that will allow your company to find and hire a perfect staff member—not just for today but for the entire life cycle of the company. To describe an employee's Vector with regard to the business, we use a company Vector. We examine their own values, momentum, future goals, and skills to understand how they can best partner with us. For small- and medium-sized enterprises, the founder's Vector is synonymous with the company Vector. In this case, we can determine how close the direction of an employee's Vector is to the company Vector, as well as how consistent life values and beliefs of an employee are with the corporate philosophy.

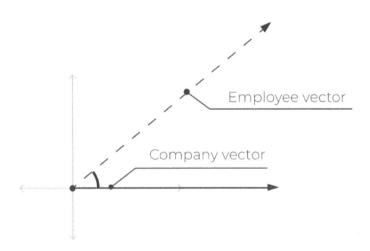

The employee's **Vector Length** represents his or her skills. Today, it is easy to determine the skills of an employee. HR departments surpass many universities in the development of tests for concentration, quick wit, knowledge of language, and technical details for any profession.

To assess skills at EnCata, all applicants are invited to undergo testing. Such tests are prepared by unit managers, and they provide the first distinct impression of the individual. Our tests allow for you to adjust the difficulty based on the employee's tenure (i.e., junior, midcareer, and senior). However, determination of the length of the

Vector is the easiest stage toward a perfect employee who meets all company's principles and targets.

The **Vector Length** can be changed with relatively little effort. Skills can easily be built with training programs or educational benefits for career-minded individuals. Generally, the courses for specialized occupations with additional in-house education can solve a problem with regard to skills improvement.

These skill-building measures serve as fertilizer for a fruitful crop, but there's more to farming than just laying down some manure. Crops need adequate light, the correct temperature, and regular hydration to grow. The length of the Vector isn't the only value needed for success; there is also the **Angle**. This is perhaps the most complex stage in selecting applicants but ensures the ones you hire will stay with the company throughout its journey.

We consider the **Angles** of future employees only within a certain framework—each manager personally evaluates them. This is determined through multiple interviews held between the manager and the applicant.

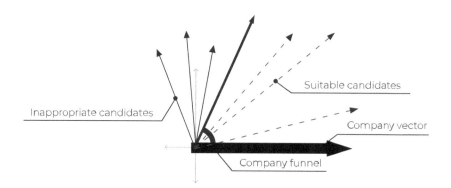

For determining the Angle, we create four points between the range of 0 and 90 degrees (no one falling in the 90-to-180-degree range is considered for employment, as they would be damaging to the company). This is how we determine an employee's Angle, or their day-to-day engagement in work. These points are homegrown for each company, and it's how you can determine the position of future staff members. If an employee's direction is opposite to the company's Vector, they are rejected immediately.

Our four points were created through a number of methods, and we annually assess them to see if they're still true to our Vector. We then judge how the employee's current trajectory maps out to our own. Changing an employee's Angle is possible, but every company must have a different approach to doing so. At EnCata, we have our own. Each organization will need to determine how to create their own methods of adjusting Angles.

In certain cases, the costs of changing an employee's Angle may not justify the result. At our current stage of development, we focus exclusively on the change of the Vector Angle, as it is more difficult to change an employee's engagement than his or her efficiency. That is why our framework of employment capabilities has narrowed so much that the applicants almost become indistinguishable from the evangelists in the company.

Changing the Angle of an employee's Vector is difficult. I've experienced this firsthand. Over the last five years, I have spent hundreds of man-hours changing the Vector of one of our key designers. We had a number of face-to-face interviews. I applied multiple methods for changing his Vector and eventually succeeded. But does it benefit the company when its chief executive officer spends his time with an individual instead of working with projects or other staff members? Yes, it does. The efficiency of a CEO spending just a single hour with the employee raises the stakes for the employee and makes them feel they have more to contribute to the company than they had previously thought.

Experience shows that a like-minded and like-aimed person can always grow into a top-performing professional. It is sometimes much more difficult to find a kindred soul in an established professional. These key employees are small boats moving downstream in the same direction as the company cruiser moves. Once the current changes, the small boats follow the current change while the larger cruiser firmly continues to follow its own route. Thus, those employees who are established already in the company with proven loyalty tie their boats to the cruiser with a chain, ensuring their mutual destination despite the seaways and currents.

When we expect that a future staff member will be our kind of exemplary employee, they should undergo a probation period lasting one month. A 360 evaluation of the employee is done at the end of the first year. This evaluation is determined by the insights of the managers, fellow staff members, and HR departments. These are critical steps that reveal additional variables in a person's Vector. In the next chapters, I will try to describe the importance of these steps, as well as the methods for working with them.

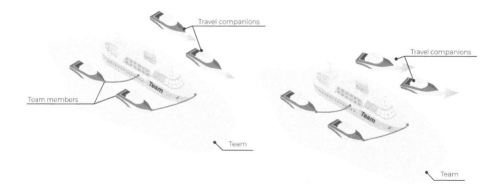

TIPS

1. Always apply employee Vector methodologies during employment of new staff and for the assessment of already-employed personnel.

2. Do your best to employ staff who are the most loyal to your company, business sector, and field of activities.

3. Provide conditions for a favorable environment in your company, since it will contribute to the management of Vectors of the employed staff.

4. Assess even the Vectors of the established experts.

CHAPTER 5

THE VECTOR IN FAMILY AND FRIENDSHIP

Finding friends when you are young can be easier than when you're an adult. We were all put in the aquarium of school with thousands of other fish to learn to swim in a synchronized fashion. Our schools organized sporting events, field trips, and school dances to encourage us to socialize. Throughout this, we created groups that shared similar goals and desires. We bonded and formed squads of friends usually not exceeding ten in number.

But when the teachers were gone and we were left to our own unfettered devices, the freedom became exhilarating for us. We now swam by ourselves, seeking others of like mind and intellect. Cultural and ethnic undertows also played a factor in our herd mentality. While at first this was exciting, as adults, this freedom can cause incredible angst.

But what about friendship? In school, we were taught this was one of the most important things to hold on to. Outside of school, we struggle to keep alive friendships that have run through their life cycle. We doggedly hang on to friends who no longer fit into our current lives or plans for the future. It is the same for an employee who no longer fits into the Vector of your organization. The Vector and its Angle will show you that these **Disintegrators** must be marginalized to allow us to continue our journey through life without anchors weighing us down.

The Vector reminds us that we must be in harmony in friendship. If it means drifting back in time, talking about days gone by, then so be it. But friendships also must serve the present day. Living our memories again is fine, but living in the past is not. As our Angles in life pivot, do not stay chained to the past with near-death friendships. Time, as we all know, is fleeting. Trying to drag friends from the past and integrate them into our world today causes stress and friction as we try to find our true personal Vector. If a friend from the past has become a **Disintegrator**—someone who detracts from your true Vector—then it's best to not include them in your new harmonious life.

If we are aware of true group Vectors like those of companies and organizations, let us seek out or gravitate toward prospective friends who can add to our happiness instead of lessen it. New apps offer programs that match friends instead of romantic partners. These individuals are matched based on interests and more. These apps have had great success with young professionals seeking new friendships. And this shows our human instinct to gravitate toward like-minded people who share the same Angle of our personal Vector.

The **Vector Funnel** is the flexibility, or meeting point, of all Vectors in an organization. Like a scatter plot, it maps out the big movements of groups of people. These meeting apps help us better understand how people coalesce in groups. We all subliminally gravitate to people with like needs and interests. Why not take this to the next level and use the Vector to minimize time in finding meaningful friendships?

I often hear older people say, "I have enough friends and don't need any new ones." To me, this sounds like the beginning of the end. This pandemic lockdown has forever changed our thoughts on the family unit. We were all tested by it; one phrase that may ring true is "familiarity breeds contempt." We all had to retool our close relationships and work with the best of our family's and friends' characteristics and try to block out or tolerate each other's shortcomings. If you hide yourself away from the world or new experiences, you stifle your own personal growth. What happens when the friends you made decades ago begin to pass away? The world is already tough enough as it is. Folks with this insulated mindset are only circling their wagons closer and closer and, in turn, making their world smaller and smaller. This leads to depression and other maladies that can rob them of their golden years.

Harmony at home is the foundation for a sane and productive life. Living a helter-skelter existence with no strategy or thought-out plans can lead to chaos and stress as well as financial miscalculations. But should a family implement a business planning strategy to smooth out the chaos? Absolutely! The family Vector must guide us all. Families can do it instinctively or with each member playing their role.

The Gravitator is often the father, who in traditional family life is the "strong man" of the family unit. The father as Gravitator does not necessarily mean that all is well at home. Yes, he may have strong energy, but he can also drive a family into despair—the same way an erratic CEO could with his company. More important on the home front is the **Integrator**—oftentimes the mother—who promotes harmony and draws the team together.

That being said, gender roles are changing every day. In America, more and more women are taking on the role of Gravitator by providing for their families. And many men are staying at home in order to harmonize and guide the familial unit. But who are the Disintegrators in the family unit? These are the children, who must be steered to the family Vector. They can be pulled by the Gravitator and taught by the Integrator. All must feel the **Gravity** of the family unit! Most disruption by the young comes in spats that are often smoothed over quickly and are just speed bumps in a family's life.

BUSINESSES INSTINCTIVELY DRIVE EMPLOYEES TO WORK TOGETHER TO FURTHER THE PROFITS AND GOALS OF THE FIRM. WHEN THERE IS A COMMON GOAL, IT IS EASY FOR A GROUP OF PEOPLE TO WORK TOGETHER.

Like a corporation that grows and becomes more complex, the extended family tree can create incredible stress and conflict for all of its members. Corporations are driven by the leader and the Vector with all of its Angles. Businesses instinctively drive employees to work together to further the profits and goals of the firm. When there is a common goal, it is easy for a group of people to work together. This is not the case with the extended family, where desires, needs, and relationships are woven together in a complicated mess of knots.

Your brothers, sisters, aunts, uncles, cousins, grandparents, and more make for a dizzying kaleidoscope of clashing Angles. There is no common thread besides family heritage. There is no driving need to work together to support each other. Besides those living under one roof, interaction in the clan is mostly voluntary, with huge clashes between relatives of different generations. The clan Vector is wide open and only comes into focus at certain times of interaction. **Mass Effect**—the movement or migration of multiple people in a group— can splinter a large, diversified extended family.

We all know the Gravitators who pull us together for reunions or the Integrators who make it all happen to keep the family group connected. Sadly, however, most of us can painfully point to the Disintegrators, who get hammered at family functions and cause turmoil. These troublemakers have no inducement to flow to the Angle (individuals' willingness to subordinate themselves to the betterment of the group). They cause mischief at all times and do not heed the Gravitators.

But why should they? The familial Vector doesn't benefit them or their trajectory. At best, these Disintegrators are family drunks who cause a scene. At worst, they can rip a family apart with their antics.

What to do with these malcontents? Talk to these Disintegrators, and do not let them stray from the **Vector Funnel**. These difficulties are natural for sure but can be solved by adhering strongly to the Vector philosophy.

CHAPTER 6

VECTOR ON THE WORLD STAGE

Throughout history, we have seen leaders, governments, and nations rise and fall. Countries have been guided by benevolent leaders or despicable despots ruling over them since the beginning of recorded time. These people have been led by their own missions, passions, needs, and wants. In short, every president, prime minister, or dictator has been guided by their Vector. Whether they are controlling their populace with an iron fist or letting them govern themselves, their Vector is omnipresent in their leadership. When these Vectors are passed down to a mass of people, they become larger than a mission— they become a system of thought.

These Vector systems have formed countries and religions. If we observe them objectively, we can see how they create life cycles for governing institutions. Many great leaders in history have started their pushes for power or influence as Disintegrators. They disrupt the Vectors of existing governments and regimes because they believe they must be changed. As they grow in influence, these agents of change become Integrators—gathering followers to help spread their own Vector. The best leaders recruit and manage their own Integrators to control how the Vector is established and measured for their belief system. However, not all these systems last.

To understand how these Vector systems fail, we only need to look east. Soviet Communism is a classic example of a failed Vector ideology that expanded quickly and died just as fast. At the start, the Bolsheviks were disruptors, attacking the existing Czarist regime. Lenin was a Gravitator, surrounded by these disruptors, but he also had the ability to attract Integrators to run the future Communist machine. Trotsky, Stalin, and other Communist leaders leveraged their organizational skills to galvanize the masses of Soviet citizens. They utilized the **Mass Effect** of these people to encourage and uplift the members of the proletariat. Despite these strengths, however, Communism's Vector was unsustainable in its practical application.

To best answer why Communism failed would take many more books than just this one. When it comes to the Vector philosophy, I believe Communism failed for not accepting any deviation from their Vector. They ruled their citizenry harshly without any flexibility in completing their mission. They didn't allow the Vector Funnel to grow and change as its citizenry did. The growth of the Vector stalled out approximately sixty years into the Soviet regime, which led to its eventual collapse and decay. And when the thaw came, there was no clear Gravitator at the helm. This dealt the final blow to the Soviet Union and its Communist utopia.

On the other hand, being too flexible in a Vector isn't always the best bet. Democracies might last longer than dictatorships, but their Vectors are not as strong. In a democracy, every election brings in a new set of Integrators who run a government. This means the Vector Funnel is always being tested by a new group and new energies.

However, this constant testing of the Vector hamstrings its growth. Disruptors flash onto the scene and are hoisted into power at mind-numbing speed. We saw this in the election of Donald Trump. The constant rollover of leadership ensures that the Vector cannot overpower the system. This safety mechanism, however, comes at the cost of rapid growth through Mass Effect.

IN A DEMOCRACY, EVERY ELECTION BRINGS IN A NEW SET OF INTEGRATORS WHO RUN A GOVERNMENT. THIS MEANS THE VECTOR FUNNEL IS ALWAYS BEING TESTED BY A NEW GROUP AND NEW ENERGIES.

There are countless historical examples of powerful Gravitators whose Vector fades into obscurity after their death. Unfortunately, most of these are because their successors do not have the ability to grow the Mass Effect of the regime before them. They just lack the charisma and motivation of the previous Gravitator. However, if they are surrounded by Integrators from the previous generation, success is almost guaranteed. A classic case of this was the great Ottoman Empire, which ran through generations of successive sultans backed by experienced grand viziers.

Another example of Vectors not being passed down successfully is the Roman Empire. Ruled by the initial Gravity of Julius and Augustus Caesar, the Roman Empire started off strong. They built upon the Vector of the Roman Republic, changing it from a democracy to a dictatorship. This changed the Vector Length as it grew their borders exponentially. However, the buck stopped at Caesar. As good emperors were followed by bad emperors, the power of the empire's Vector began to wane, and the empire eventually imploded. The Vector of the empire was so strong, however, that the decline and fall took over four hundred years. At their borders, they began to feel the pressure of new Gravitators on all sides. These roaming empires of the Huns and Goths pressed in on their borders and destroyed the great empire.

In recent history, we have seen the influence of these strong Gravitators and their Integrators who orchestrate the movement and dynamics of their populace. Saddam Hussein, Gaddafi, and the Ayatollah Khomeini have all led their people with a strong fist that allows for no deviation from the Vector. They knew that if they did, their regimes would collapse. Strict leadership, however, is not always a sign of a failed regime. In fact, if these types of leaders can provide a good standard of living for their citizens, they could inspire great loyalty and pride in their country. If they cannot, their fall from power would be brutal and quick.

When American-led democracies clash with dictatorships, the results are often catastrophic. These democratic countries try to move the Vector of dictatorships after doing away with their leaders. These underdeveloped countries, however, are not well suited for this massive Vector change. By eliminating the leader and their inner circle, these invading forces destroy the Gravitators of the regime. This results in a chaos where Disintegrators thrive.

Regime change is possible, albeit much more difficult than the United States leads us to believe. Dictatorships cannot be eradicated simply by installing a new leader. It is a long process that requires creativity and mercy. If the United States wants to change world democracy, they must listen to the people they're liberating. They must encourage a Vector change without forcing it. They must have the compassion to act and the courage to listen to what is needed.

It will be fascinating to observe world leaders as Gravitators for their respective countries. During this pandemic "reset," governments are strained beyond capacity in their ability to support their citizens' needs. Nations' Vectors will be monumentally challenged and reshaped. Many world leaders are being lashed by their citizens as health systems have failed and countries are overwhelmed by the pandemic and its fallout. World leaders must understand the Vectors of their countries and work to achieve a semblance of compliance with them. Governments will fall, leaders will be replaced, and the world will be reset as the Gravitators move to their respective countries' Vectors.

CHAPTER 7

THE FOUNDER'S VECTOR

The key to understanding the Vector philosophy is to focus on the founder's Vector whenever possible. That being said, their dreams and goals can't be impossible-to-reach aspirations. The company Vector demands an objective assessment of the founder's vision and how it can be achieved through the work of the organization. How a founder deals with the day-to-day of an organization shows their character and personality. Founders deal with big issues that sometimes cause them to take on eccentric behavior.

For example, a wealthy businessman buys an island just to throw an exclusive staff party every couple of quarters. He also tries to cross the Atlantic in a small boat to prove a point to a colleague, only to be capsized midtrip. After he's fished out of the ocean, he wastes no time devising a scheme to cross the Pacific—this time in a red hot-air balloon. Later, when he loses another bet with a peer, he takes on the uniform of his employees to cater to the passengers flying his airline. These, and many more, are the antics of Richard Branson, founder of the Virgin Group. He is a vivid example of how the image of a founder in the public's eye can influence the operations and branding of a company. This energy, however, can be dangerous when experienced by an individual.

In a smaller organization, the founder's role has the greatest sway. Day in and day out, the founder communicates personally with lower-level employees. At this stage of the organization's life cycle, the company's Vector is virtually indistinguishable from the founder's Vector. They determine both business policy and growth areas for employees.

In smaller companies the founder's role is amplified. The more employees the founder communicates personally with, the greater their influence on the team—it comes from them setting examples that become the company's philosophy. At this early stage, the influence of the founder is so great that the company's Vector is hardly distinguishable from the founder's Vector. It determines both the business policy and the growth area for the employees. As the organization grows, however, the company's Vector must shift. More and more employees mean different missions and goals. In order to achieve stability, the company must have a stable philosophy based on the ideals of the founder.

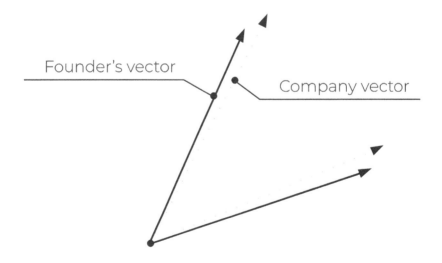

Founder's vector

Company vector

But a founder is still just a person. And they're going to have their personal ups and downs. Steve Jobs and Elon Musk were known for eccentric outbursts that brought chaos into their organizations. These giants, however, aren't exceptions. Even simple proximity to the founder can have unpredictable consequences on employees below them, leading to burnout and overburdening.

Imagine that a company is like a solar system. The founder is the sun, and orbiting around them are the employees as planets. At an appropriate distance, employees receive a sufficient amount of energy from the founder to be self-sustainable. If an employee is pulled too close to the founder without proper preparation, they will be bombarded with the founder's energy—big-picture ideas and massive organizational shifts. Unequipped to deal with this level of organizational operations, the employee will feel burned out and move further away from the founder and the organization's Vector.

Burnout is a widespread disease that has infected companies of all sizes. Today, employees yearn to be a key player. They desire to do well and contribute to their team. In their efforts to do so, however, they take on too much. At first, this is energizing but before long becomes stressful and overwhelming. Soon, each new task is no longer seen as an opportunity but rather an annoyance. They become jaded and indifferent, which makes it even harder to encourage them in their work.

In order to combat this problem at EnCata, we monitor our employees monthly to make sure we're catching burnout at its earliest stages. Every month, management meets with the CEO (in our case, the founder) to assess each employee's key performance indicators (**KPIs**) to check on their experience at the company. These **KPIs** are unique to EnCata, but, when combating burnout at your company, you should follow these tips:

1. **Review the employee's workload.** If an employee's task list continues to grow and deliverables are way past due, it may be a sign of the employee's growing frustration with the firm.

2. **Evaluate the employee's time management.** If an employee is always snowed under with work or consistently procrastinating, these could be signs they are not using their time wisely.

3. **Check in on the employee's commitment.** If an employee repeatedly shows negativity toward their tasks or believes there is nothing of interest in their work, it proves low commitment.

4. **Assess the employee's health and wellness.** Is your employee showing signs of sleep deprivation, depression, or some other physical instability? These kinds of symptoms can make it difficult for them to perform work-related tasks, even if they have every desire to contribute to their team.

When an immediate subordinate is suffering from burnout, their manager must know the reason why so they can take action. If the burnout continues, the employee's Vector will change, and the termination process will begin. This is why steps should be taken early to prevent losing a valuable asset in accomplishing the company's Vector. And the best way to keep employees on track is to ensure their Vector reflects that of the company. Changing an employee's Vector is a solid way to prevent professional burnout. This change can be either urgent or long term.

Urgent change of job function is the fastest and most effective way to solve the problem for both employee and company. If an employee feels they aren't contributing, it is vital that you give them a task that they feel like they can succeed in. If they are given a task that they think is below them, they feel useless and will grow more resentful. And under no circumstances should pay or benefits be cut due to burnout. This is a surefire way to make the situation even worse.

At EnCata, our management is well prepared to address the matter of burnout. We did this by appointing a burnout survivor as a high-level company manager. We also prevent burnout by giving stressed-out employees a chance to develop themselves in new fields. Finally, we make sure that salary level doesn't change due to burnout. Today, that burnout survivor is one of the top leaders in our business and an example of how the Vector system can pull even the most exhausted employees out of a funk. They're reinvigorated and have created a new and exciting career for themselves.

Once the employee is redirected into new and meaningful work, we introduce a range of strategies to reactivate the disengaged employee. Here are some of the steps we use to fight burnout:

1. **Limit the number of tasks for an employee.** Let them close a few tasks pending in the "to-do" list. Once they are able to cross them off the list, the recovery will start. Make sure you point out their success. Even the most insignificant and nonmonetary praise can be more meaningful than financial bonuses.

2. **Find a task that the employee has been yearning for, and let them dive in.** Never mind if this task is not the most important and urgent—otherwise, work procrastination will require much more wasted energy by the company.

3. **Settle as many anxiety-inducing situations as possible.** It is continuous stress that negatively impacts the quality of an employee's work.

4. **Allow the employee to delegate some of their tasks.** If they keep getting behind, talk to their supervisors, and assist in clearing up their workload.

5. **Demonstrate supervisors' confidence in the employee.** Give them the support they need from a managerial perspective.

6. **Convince them to spend more off time outside.** At least half an hour of their lunch break should be spent outside the office to shift attention and release anxiety.

7. **Encourage them to take care of their physical and mental well-being.** Many companies cover the costs of gyms and fitness clubs.

There is one last way to fight burnout: dismissal. As hard as it is to admit, sometimes it is the right move for both the individual and the company. Burned-out employees often feel trapped. They think there are no other options for them. They yearn to be free and realize their true potential. At times like these, dismissal helps them fulfill themselves outside the company. Businesses can waste years on skills training or conveying the company philosophy, but often, it won't change that employee's Vector.

It is worth mentioning that burnout can happen to anyone. From frontline employees to managers and even CEOs, anyone whose Vector is affected by the Vector of the company is subject to burnout. This is why so many founders delegate management to their staff.

An example—a dynamic CEO of a worldwide tech firm was bogged down by managing his fifty thousand employees. For twenty years, he had built the organization brick by brick, growing their company's footprint to reach thirty countries. Despite the forward momentum, however, he was finding himself less and less effective each month. He was spreading himself too thin across the firm. Once he realized this, he limited his access to twenty key employees who would help him focus on larger issues. Almost immediately, he found that his productivity had greatly increased, while his anxiety over work had melted away. Since work had settled down for him, he could focus more on personal matters at home.

Another young, hardworking founder discovered that most of his day was dedicated to making hundreds of small decisions that were vital to the company. While these decisions needed to be made, they became a drag on his time and prevented him from driving the company forward. He was lost in the day-to-day and needed to be thinking about the larger strategy.

Quickly, the CEO brought in a president who was a proven business veteran. They trained the new expert on the inner workings of the company and then left him to his own devices. This new president operated the business as he saw fit—without adapting to the founder's vision. Before long, the business was on the rocks, veering closer and closer to bankruptcy. Who's at fault for this unfortunate situation? All of them. All parties were guilty of not following the Vector of the company!

At times, a founder's Vector and position can change for more objective reasons. At each stage of a company's development, the firm should always be on the lookout for new managers that suit the current stage of the organization's life cycle. In the early stages of a start-up, a founder may opt for a more authoritarian management style in order to pursue a specific goal. That tight grip, however, cannot stay clenched for long. The founder will have to think about a smart company management system and how they can disengage from this approach when needed. Having a strong but flexible Vector is key to understanding when this shift is needed.

In today's world, a business leader must be driven by promptness, purposefulness, and intuition, the combination of which creates a natural Gravity that draws in hard workers and dedicated employees. Without all these qualities, it is impossible to create a Vector of the company or to find anyone to have faith in it. Faith in the founder and loyalty to the company are basic premises that turn the company's employees into evangelists. These are evangelists who start each and every day with true inspiration and a smile on their face.

TIPS

1. Do not forget that the company founder is not only an example for the employees but also the main factor, determining the Vector of the business.

2. Close interaction between the founder and the employee over a long period of time can lead to unpredictable consequences—burnout is one of them.

3. Burnout should be fought in various ways. If an immediate result is required, a measured plan must be implemented to change the Vector of the burned-out employee.

4. A specific manager style must meet the company requirements at each stage of its growth. Founders must understand when it is best to delegate oversight to a more skilled manager in that area of operation.

CHAPTER 8

VECTOR EVALUATION

These days, society is filled with stereotypes that influence how we make our day-to-day decisions. We consider ourselves happy when there's a specific number of zeros after a comma in our personal bank accounts. Many of us believe our children must graduate from good academic institutions in order to achieve career success. I believe there is nothing wrong with these stereotypes. In fact, they can help motivate us to accomplish our goals. Some stereotypes, however, can be harmful and provide us with false information.

We often see the world as chaos, where happenstance can lead to mayhem for our personal lives. We try to blame our personal failures on the chaos that the world thrives on. We let ourselves be consumed by this chaos and distract us from our true calling. Every action we take can be tinged with guilt as we try to confront issues that are beyond our control. Despite all this, there are still people with clear vision that helps them understand their own personal goals and the actions needed to accomplish them. Thanks to individuals like this, I was able to implement the Vector theory within EnCata. More importantly, these individuals helped me understand the structures of the world around me. What I used to see as chaos, I now see as an orderly process that I can control.

One of the most integral members of the EnCata team is an engineer who has many symptoms of autism. This employee performs his duties with incredible accuracy. Many might see his perspective as a disability, but his unique makeup has helped him focus on his daily tasks and achieve outstanding results. He has achieved his professional goals and has set a shining example for other employees. Moreover, he's a Gravitator who brings them together and makes everyone—including myself—a little bit better. These few lines are not dedicated to the fight against discrimination in the workplace or support of the disabled. Like this whole book, they are dedicated to business, whose primary task is to bring profit to the company, the owner, and society. That is why selection of employees is done through a specific Funnel.

THE VECTOR IN ACTION

The unique nature of the EnCata philosophy calls for seeking professionals and those willing to work in the "spirit" of the company. Today, all personnel decisions are made by the company's partners and heads of departments. Heads of departments make up an order to seek out a new employee with specific skills, and the search begins. We get about one hundred résumés for each vacancy. We then carry out twenty to thirty telephone interviews, which result in ten first meetings. After those meetings, we cut the list down to five for the second round and eventually two to three candidates for a trial day. Only one stays for a trial month. This sole employee goes through the Funnel that took us years to build. When a candidate gets to an interview with our HR partner for the first time, their Vector has already been determined and the opinions of the partners and colleagues of the future employee analyzed.

It should be noted that we will make an offer to the candidate only if their Vector gets into our Funnel. In case of nonalignment, there is no point in company wasting time and changing the Vector of the potential employee. It is extremely time consuming, and time is our most valuable resource. Less energy is required to change one's professional qualities compared to changing the Angle of a Vector. Personality traits are established through education and upbringing. These can be incredibly difficult traits to accomplish. For example, it's not easy to get an employee to clean up their workstation if their mother cleaned up the scattered LEGO they played with as a child.

If, for example, you are working on a supersonic aircraft project and evaluate this rather complex task, you need to calculate the number of man-hours and the amount of material required. Most commonly these tasks are not well performed if management is not in alignment with the employees. However, if a team tries to analyze each node separately, the aircraft will become a realistic project with a specific deadline. When you evaluate and add up each node of the aircraft, you will get a value fairly similar to the real design with understandable indexes.

This process is like measuring a person's Vector and their basic moral and ethical principles. When you try to change a person's Vector, you are changing everything in their culture, their upbringing, and their values, but if you change one thing at a time, you can shift it. It is difficult, but it is not impossible to change. Moreover, in this book you will find examples of how we changed the Vector. Because it is difficult, we must understand when and in what situations it will be reasonable to change the Vector.

VECTOR LOYALTY AND THE FUNNEL

While working, you will keep investing efforts and means in employee efficiency growth (the Vector Length), but also in changing their loyalty (the Vector Angle). This work can take years. Note that if the

Angle deviates from the Funnel and shows as negative, the employee's activity in the company will do more damage than good. If there is no Funnel, the employee's Angle will inevitably show up in the company.

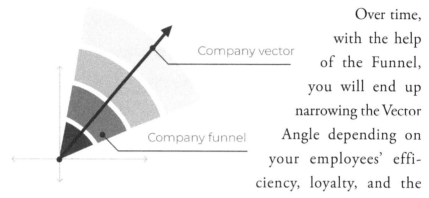

Over time, with the help of the Funnel, you will end up narrowing the Vector Angle depending on your employees' efficiency, loyalty, and the existing labor market. Before long you will not evaluate people by personal efficiency but rather consider information on the candidate's Vector and their whereabouts in your Funnel.

GALLOPING GROWTH

Often businesses find themselves in galloping growth conditions. This is a great problem to have! Being supporters of accelerated growth, we have prepared a solution for companies dealing with this rapid development. First off, let's discuss the constraint of staff expansion. Even if you need an employee here and now, by hiring them, you run the risk that their presence will have a negative impact on the rest of the team. In this situation it is better to stop at the edge of the Funnel, so that the total Gravity of the team does not go beyond it. This is a complex process, and the result can be extremely controversial. However, risks can be reduced by evaluating the candidate's Vector. Evaluation of the candidate's Vector can be done with the help of the technique that allows determination of the actual Vector of each person.

Each supervisor and HR specialist has the experience of working with a large number of people. To some extent, this gives them the ability to determine a person's efficiency and predilection. The more interviews you carry out, the better you will understand whether this person suits you or not.

RISKS CAN BE REDUCED BY EVALUATING THE CANDIDATE'S VECTOR. EVALUATION OF THE CANDIDATE'S VECTOR CAN BE DONE WITH THE HELP OF THE TECHNIQUE THAT ALLOWS DETERMINATION OF THE ACTUAL VECTOR OF EACH PERSON.

Psychology is an extremely complex science. Not every HR professional is able to see all the variables that influence and affect a person's inner workings. Even upon collecting and analyzing opinions of their colleagues, a decision about hiring will still remain subjective. Despite the method of Vector evaluation being rather conventional, we try to make it as accurate as possible by breaking it into smaller tasks. These tasks have been created to evaluate the following criteria.

VECTOR AND EMPLOYEE LOYALTY

We have selected three common and standard gradations for employee evaluation: junior, middle, and senior. We have also added a percentage scale to this system to determine the level within the gradation itself. This system reflects the length of the employee Vector.

GRADATION TABLE

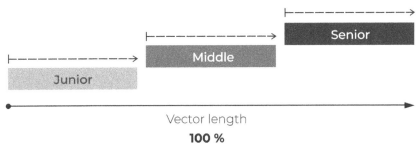

Senior

Middle

Junior

Vector length
100 %

The Angle detection system is the immediate supervisor's task to determine the employee's loyalty. The manager will make a decision based on three to five parameters. Without a doubt, the employee cannot run his or her life only thinking of the company. Therefore, the maximum loyalty remains unattainable. However, the actual values between –90 and +90 degrees show how close the employee is to the highest value. After that, all the employees can be evaluated, as well as their total Vector sum, which will show an objective loyalty picture for employees across the firm.

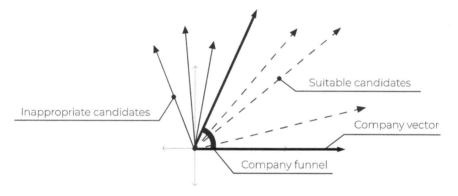

Many people wonder how to accurately determine an employee's loyalty, given that human parameters are nearly impossible to compare with mathematical values. In fact, it is possible to evaluate each candidate and the company's activity as a whole. That's the point of the technique: evaluating the effectiveness of the whole company by trying to identify the efficiency of each employee. Vector evaluation is the work of specific supervisors who carry out a monthly evaluation of their employees. Upper management evaluates the supervisors, and upward it flows.

We experimented with Vector evaluation by allowing completely different supervisors to evaluate the work of other employees. Moreover, we conducted cross-evaluation: heads of other departments gave their opinions on the supervisors in another division. It turned out that evaluation of all managers was almost identical. No doubt, each manager's opinion was subjective, but the overall assessment was accurate according to our data. This way we have come to understand the efficiency and productivity of each employee at EnCata.

Sounds complicated? Not at all. Here is a way you can evaluate even more abstract characteristics of a person. Gather a group of people off the street, and have another group judge their beauty. It's important that the group doing the judging is from a similar culture. You will begin to realize how the focus group will coalesce around specific beauty criteria and assign value to seemingly meaningless visual data. The human brain can only evaluate. It takes in complex data sets—such as attractiveness—as a measurable value and makes a comparison.

LEMONS AND ORANGES

In 1970, American economist George Akerlof made a splash in economic science by publishing an article called "The Market of Lemons." In the article, he explored the troubles a buyer faces when choosing a second-hand car in the market. Akerlof posited that every secondhand car could either be defined as a lemon or an orange. A "lemon" was a car that had defects that were discovered only after the purchase. "Oranges" were cars that were technically in good condition—before and after buying. The article went on to posit that there were lemons and oranges in almost every buying situation in economics. They thought that there were many potential reasons for the "oranges" being driven from the market by "lemons." In 2001, Akerlof and his coauthors won the Nobel Prize in economics for this study.

We have applied the main theses of this study in regard to the personnel policy. For us there are also lemons and oranges in the labor market. To us, lemons are experienced candidates who overestimate their abilities and raise demands they need us to meet. Oranges, on the contrary, evaluate themselves adequately and accept the conditions created by the company. Like in any other company, the first stages of the EnCata development had to do with lemons. We evaluated the market, considered the candidates, and adopted their experience. Over time, we added "orange juice" to their "lemon juice" through training and corporate philosophy. Through these tactics, we turned these lemons into oranges. Thanks to this approach, we can offer our employees the most comfortable working conditions.

THERE ARE ALSO LEMONS AND ORANGES IN THE LABOR MARKET. TO US, LEMONS ARE EXPERIENCED CANDIDATES WHO OVERESTIMATE THEIR ABILITIES AND RAISE DEMANDS THEY NEED US TO MEET. ORANGES, ON THE CONTRARY, EVALUATE THEMSELVES ADEQUATELY AND ACCEPT THE CONDITIONS CREATED BY THE COMPANY.

Today, we continue to improve the system of candidate evaluation and narrow the future employee selection Funnel. In order to do so, we often ignore contemporary trends in HR. We consider both the situation in the market and the internal needs of the company. We take into account the needs and desires of each employee we hire and ensure that they continue to grow within the Vector of our company. By following our example, you can grow your own workforce into a team of devoted employees who help you attain your company's goals.

TIPS

1. Split complex tasks into several simple ones.

2. HR is paramount to business. Only entrust Vector assessment to HR partners and departments with which you work closely and that you can control.

3. Take into account not only the candidate's efficiency (Vector Length), but also his or her loyalty to the company (Vector Angle).

4. Implement the evaluation of the candidate's Vector based on the existing recruitment funnel.

5. Create an "orange" team. To "buy" employees more expensive than the labor market without looking back at the Vector Angle is not the best solution for the company.

CHAPTER 9

GRAVITY AND INTEGRATION

Have you ever been to Kolkata (formerly known as Calcutta)? Neither have I, but I have heard it described as a destitute city covered in trash and filth. A first-time visitor to the city will be shocked at what they find underfoot. Native Kolkatans, however, do not see a problem and throw their own trash into the streets and waterways. In Minsk, it is almost the extreme opposite. Every day, citizens enjoy almost perfect cleanliness on the streets because the citizenry is constantly cleaning up after themselves.

When we find ourselves in a completely new environment—especially one outside of our comfort zone—we try to either adapt or change it. Most choose to adapt. It's neither bad nor good; it is a reality that businesses should accept and integrate into its processes.

In the previous chapters, you may have noticed such terms as **Gravity** and **Integration**. They sound natural and understandable in the context of human relations. In this chapter, I will explain more fully these terms and how they relate to creating your Vector-forward organization. I've always relied on physics to explain what's going on around me. If something is unclear to me, I rationalize it using the laws of physics. With my collaborator, Rod, we even developed a special formula to write this book. Our intention is to look at human relations and how groups of people congregate and disperse in a way that reflects the laws of physics that govern our natural world.

GRAVITY IN ALL PHASES OF OUR EXISTENCE

I sincerely believe that everything around us operates on a physical basis. Imagine, for a moment, that the Gravity acceleration of our planet changed by 10 percent. Everything around us would change: economics, psychology, and yes, even human relations. That is why Gravity plays such an important role in my work. It is one of the most significant natural phenomena and a foundation in the law of attraction. This law states that bodies with a similar force and weight are attracted to each other, but bodies with less weight will be attracted to bodies with more weight. In fact, the increase in mass of one body will influence the inertia of another body with less mass. This change in inertia can cause a change in Vector of an object. This phenomenon is not only present in the stars and planets, but within groups of people as well. Each person has his or her own Gravity—a feature reflecting the ability to attract other people and change their Vector Angles and their outlook.

Gravity is a human characteristic. Over a lifetime, only a few people can slightly increase their attraction. Therefore, there will be no universal tips on how to improve your Gravity and start creating a natural environment around you. If you have very few friends and they would rather watch another Netflix show than go out with you, you can do nothing to change that. End of story.

THE GRAVITATOR

Take a look at ringleaders in any team. Starting from a very early age, these folks take charge when they're in a group of people. Normally, such people become entrepreneurs. They lead the way for others and reflect the Vector of a whole company. In the hiring process, you can see an employee's gravitational extremes within a month of employment. You

GRAVITATORS BECOME ANCHORS WHO ARE ABLE TO PULL VECTORS OF THE OTHER EMPLOYEES IN THEIR DIRECTION. IT IS OBVIOUS THAT A PERSON WITH STRONGER GRAVITY CHANGES VECTORS OF OTHERS.

should feel a deep interest in this person and their life. If you get little to no feeling about a potential candidate, even if they are an ideal hire, they are most likely a low-Gravity candidate. If, however, you meet an employee who feels like an old friend even though you just met, you have just met a Gravitator or an Integrator.

Today, we try to identify employees with higher Gravity in the first months of their work. In the long run, these Gravitators become anchors who are able to pull Vectors of the other employees in their direction. It is obvious that a person with stronger Gravity changes Vectors of others. Therefore, we implement loyal Gravitators in completely different teams. We also use this technique as a means to change an employee's Vector.

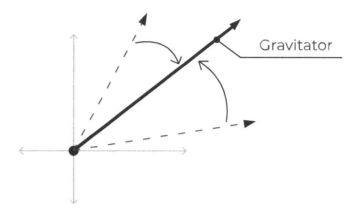

At the same time, we consider a whole range of factors that affect Gravitators themselves. A calculation of total employee Gravities can be compiled by management. Supervisors should clearly see what kind of Gravity they have on their teams and how it will affect the makeup of their teams. As an example, if there are ten employees in the office, their interaction will create a common Vector. This will influence the behaviors of a newcomer to the office. Most newcomers follow the common Gravity and adopt specific features of the group: loyalty and a level of efficiency. It's incredibly difficult for a newcomer to shift the balance on a new team. A team fears innovation, and it's difficult to get them to leave their comfort zone. This is why it's quite natural for newcomers to adapt to the status quo so their coworkers "like them."

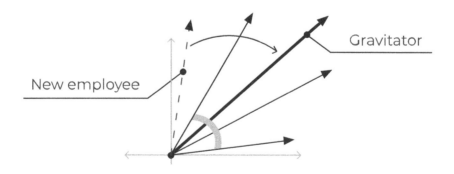

A strong Gravitator, however, will not be swayed by the impulses of the group. A strong Gravitator is capable of pulling all ten employees in his or her direction. That is why it is important for that person to be as loyal to the company as possible. This Gravity can also work in the opposite direction with a catastrophic outcome. Let's say you bring together a team of highly efficient and loyal employees with the correct Vector and then introduce an employee with a negative Vector. In the end, the strongest Gravity will turn the common team Vector—potentially against the company.

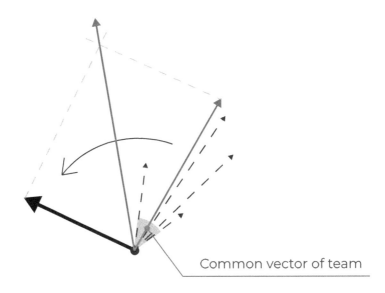

Common vector of team

Supervisors should focus on regular interaction with Gravitators to ensure they change employees' Vectors in accordance with the company Vector. Gravitators do not always become leaders. A person may well have the strongest Gravity but fails at being a leader. Such people are usually called "Mom." Only she attracts us as strongly as possible. She changes our opinions but doesn't lead the way. She is not a leader but an absolute authority and Gravitator. At the same time, Gravity is one of the most important features of a true leader. Gravity, however, can have its dark side. What we call "imaginary Gravity" can seriously affect the team and impact business growth on the whole. We will explore this concept in later chapters in this book.

EMPLOYEE INTEGRATION

In the Vector philosophy, we also use the term "Integration" separately from Gravity. This is one of the most important employee character-istics. If Gravity is the beaming sun, Integrations are the surface of the planet that absorb the light from the star. Integration is a person's ability to accelerate the processes of interaction on a team. Integra-tion allows us to fix Vectors for a synchronized change. It helps to attract people and bring them together to achieve common goals. Any good leader has both Gravity and integrational skills—they're able to influence a person through their Gravity. Even if such an employee is not a supervisor, their colleagues will still favor their requests, just because they come from these admired coworkers.

Just as the company places people of different levels of Gravity together, they must also note the integrational skills of each employee when placing them in a team. It is critical that supervisors don't place a Disintegrator on a team. Most commonly employees integrate under the influence of Gravity quite naturally, but a Disintegrator introduces extra tension between the Vectors.

THE DISINTEGRATOR

It is impossible to create a productive team without a prominent Gravi-tator and Integrator. In an incredibly weak team without these key players, an employee will emerge as a "Disintegrator"—a person who sows chaos in the team and slows down the process of interconnecting vectors. That is why Gravity and Integration should be maintained within the team at all times. Any processes in physics, philosophy, and psychology are based on the stability of the system. Therefore, the primary task of the CEO, HR partner, and HR department is to find the right employees, taking into account each person's culture and skills. After all, it's only when the entire team is unified behind a common goal that they will be capable of solving a complex issue.

We also pay special attention to the employee's ability to change the Vector. Such an ability shows if the employee(s) are ready to adopt the influence of another person's Gravity and Integration and to what extent. Today, current business tasks can change each quarter. For example, making a strategic change in plan for a start-up is like clearing out your spam folder. This many changes come too often.

Whereas employees, especially in fast-changing industries such as IT, should be ready for transformations and constant reforms. They know that they alone have to improve business processes that in turn will increase the welfare of the company. At EnCata, we have noticed that it is much easier to change entry-level workers than experienced, educated employees. Laborers make decisions based on trust and emotions. Intellectual workers, on the other hand, debate over every single choice and can often be led astray by overthinking.

SPEED OF THE VECTOR

This is why we look at the rate of the Vector change. This parameter depends on a variety of things, such as the employee's specialty, environment, and age. If the employee's previous employer was from a similar industry, the candidate's rate of Vector change will be much higher than that of an employee from a different business sector. While we in no way hire based on age, we clearly understand that changing the Vector of a sixty-year-old will be much more difficult than changing that of a twenty-year-old.

By gradually introducing this terminology when evaluating employees, we have seen our successful businesses becoming even more successful. Over the past four years, we reduced staff turnover by half and reached our goal of creating a team with a common philosophy. From hiring to dismissal, we make sure to observe and track every employee to make sure they are serving their purpose.

TIPS

1. Most employees adapt to the existing conditions.

2. Gravity is the ability to attract other people.

3. Identify Gravitators at the early stages, and work to get their loyalty.

4. Implement strong and loyal Gravitators in the teams that require change of the common Vector.

5. Integrative management is impacted on a person by Gravity to induce action.

6. Gravity and Integration should be stably maintained within a team.

7. Ability to change the Vector shows how much the employee is ready to take the influence of someone else's Gravity and Integration.

8. The rate of Vector change depends on the type of activity, environment, and age of the employee.

9. The Integrator implements strategies of the founder and makes best efforts that are accepted by the employees.

CHAPTER 10

MASS EFFECT

"An IT specialist walks into a bar and orders a smoothie …" In the past couple of chapters, we've gone over stereotyped thinking and how it can affect your business. The smoothie is an example of such stereotyped thinking when it comes to IT specialists. Almost every IT specialist I know loves this drink. Unfortunately, this type of thinking is completely flawed—especially when it comes to the IT industry.

Also, smoothies are delicious and healthy. Yet I only discovered them just recently. Just like building a business, you can choose what information you wish to accept and make your own opinion of the latest and greatest smoothie in the marketplace.

Again and again, entrepreneurs have to slap together odd groups of people to create a team. This blending together of different kinds of people can

A FAST-GROWING COMPANY CAN FORCE THE CEO TO CONSTANTLY FILL NEW REQUISITIONS. THIS CAN RESULT IN THROWING WORKERS WITH DIFFERENT SKILLS AND VECTORS INTO THE SAME TEAM, ALMOST AS IF YOU WERE BLENDING CELERY WITH BANANAS.

be disastrous at the start. The manager could lack the resources to quickly perform build and Integration tasks. A fast-growing company can force the CEO to constantly fill new requisitions. This can result in throwing workers with different skills and Vectors into the same team, almost as if you were blending celery with bananas.

After a while, the interaction of these discrete Vectors will bring the system into a state of equilibrium, thus creating a common Vector for the company. Whether or not this Vector is positive or negative for the company depends on the ingredients in the smoothie. Are they of high quality—meaning, are you hiring employees of the highest caliber? Essentially, the mass hiring of employees can have dire consequences. It could negatively impact the culture of the company and decrease overall productivity.

Imagine for a moment that your team is made up of a high school student, a college student, a worker, and a dog. After some time, of course, the system will reach an equilibrium. In this equilibrium, a new random Vector will be created. Whether or not this common Vector will be useful to the company is anyone's guess. Hopefully, the dog will not emerge as the Gravitator!

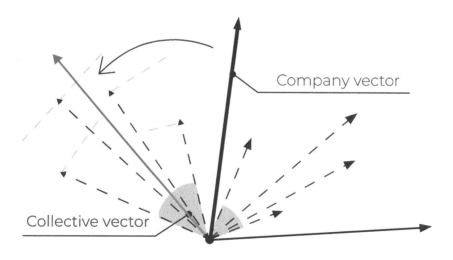

Avoiding a "negative Mass Effect" is the most important task for a growing business. In order to do so, we tested groups of new hires. We grouped them into sectors based on mass recruitment. Each group had its own level of efficiency and loyalty. This is how we derived the overall Vector of each team. We've almost never encountered the exact same indicators of Vector values. In essence, every team is unique, but trends in behavior can be observed.

In order to have an efficient system, you have to separate employees according to their parameters—separate babies from teens, college students from professionals. After that is done, you must further organize your staff into joint work groups. You must do this both to transfer experience among the group but also to form a skill assessment for the entire group. Once both the skill and the culture of the groups have achieved equilibrium, we then introduce a well-established employee with good Gravity and Vectors into the group. They serve as a kind of anchor for our candidates. We will also add more of these kinds of employees to groups that are closer to the decision-making center of the company.

Through this method, we don't just recruit employees and see what happens next. We carefully form each Vector and observe how it will interact with the others. We also look at how the Gravity of certain individuals can benefit or harm the team. From the very first day of a new team, we control these processes and do not even allow the formation of a common Vector that is unsuitable for the business.

TEAM CREATION

Carefully thinking about how you create your teams is a key stage in building your organization. We outline our key processes for team creation in a later chapter of this book. Equally important to creating the perfect team is encouraging the individual. Each manager should have a steady line of communication to each of their employees. One of the manager's key responsibilities is being able to balance the personal needs of each employee with the collective goal of the group. This is how they will affect the group Vector. These measures taken to create and influence the collective Vector will result in a positive Mass Effect—an additional opportunity for the manager to take hold of the situation.

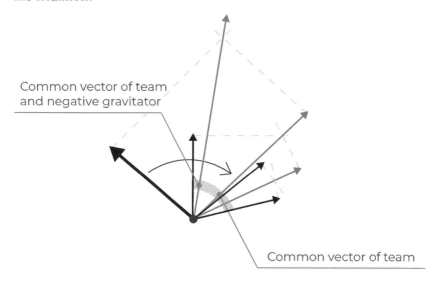

Common vector of team and negative gravitator

Common vector of team

Every newcomer to a team will be under a daily influence of the powerful Gravity that the team contains. If that Gravity is positive, it will increase their overall loyalty to the company. In turn, this will speed up their adaptation to the company and encourage them to adopt its corporate standards and philosophy. Team building is one of the most complex HR tasks for any company. For this task, you must first drink a liter of smoothies, and then you can believe it is worth it. In the worst case, you simply cut the fat in order to create the ideal employee.

TIPS

1. The interaction of employee Vectors brings the system to an equilibrium state and produces a positive or negative common collective Vector.

2. The massive unsystematic and unreasonable addition of employees to departments can lead to dire consequences.

3. In order to level the negative Mass Effect, we divide candidates into groups for the subsequent mass recruitment into specific divisions. A true Gravitator within the team is not always a leader.

4. In order to form a more or less efficient system, you need to divide employees according to certain parameters.

5. In groups, you need to add employees with well-established Vectors and Gravity, as close as possible to the Vector of the company.

6. Each group has its own specific level of efficiency and loyalty, which reflects the general Vector of the formed team.

7. A personalized approach combined with collective solutions increases the likelihood of forming a collective Vector in the same direction as the company Vector.

8. Positive Mass Effect is a powerful factor that increases employee loyalty to the company.

9. Negative Mass Effect is a powerful factor that reduces employee loyalty to the company.

CHAPTER 11

STRONG VECTOR EFFECT

If you have been an attentive reader, you will have noticed that our philosophy heavily focuses on the company founder. As mentioned in previous chapters, these people can be eccentric or strong willed. Just like the sun, they can brightly illuminate the sky and warm those who orbit them or incinerate those who get too close. I dedicate this book to those people—the ones who've been burned by the sun of a CEO. This huge life experience should be synthesized by each executive, who hopefully will incorporate best practices that will enhance their future Vectors as leaders.

In this chapter, we will take a slight detour and explore the liberty and freedom of such entrepreneurs. As an entrepreneur myself, I often find that my actions and behaviors go beyond the average man's routine. I'm hardly ever "off the clock." Instead, I'm almost always wearing my corporate shirt emblazoned with the EnCata logo. I do so because I am setting an example for every EnCata employee. It's also important to me that I am living our corporate philosophy every day. I can't ignore something that's embroidered on a shirt I wear every day! This is how I tried to convince my wife to let me wear the shirt for our family photo. I failed.

She forced me to smile at the camera in a heartless polo shirt. The myriad atoms in my body rejected the alien fabric touching it. My unnatural and lifeless smile for the photo didn't stop her attacks on my business life. My Bluetooth headset was next. Without a doubt, it was an assault on my dignity! For the last five years, I have never gone anywhere without it. Whether it was a children's performance or a glass of beer shared with friends, it was a constant part of my uniform. I needed to stay in touch! I could not be unplugged!

Any driven entrepreneur has an unquenchable thirst to work twelve to fourteen hours a day. In our constant desire to do more, we set a standard for every employee who wants to work alongside us. We are leaders that set an example, thanks to the strength of the Vector possessed by every strong-minded entrepreneur. It is the effect of this strong Vector that allows us industry leaders to establish companies and manage large businesses. Therefore, it's the founder's job to identify the strong company Vector within the first year of the company as well as identify the strong level of the employee within their first year of work.

Let us keep in mind that a strong Vector is not always positive. It can have a negative effect on your company and cause it to go out of control. In order to avoid this, supervisors should consistently interact with employees and leaders with strong Vectors. Without this connection, these folks are more likely to experience burnout. Despite their large output, these strong employees can be overworked, just like the rest of your staff. Once burnout turns their Vector into something negative, you have a Disintegrator on your

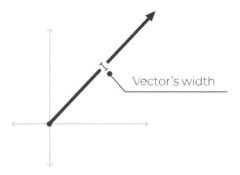

Vector's width

hands. Maintaining stability among teams is a major task of managers and leaders. They should never ignore a Vector going haywire.

VECTOR LIFE CYCLE

Each stage of a company's development demands specific skills and qualities of the main supervisors and leaders. Taking these things into account will ensure the company's rapid growth. When first starting a company off, there will be a decision vacuum. People who start companies feel they should get things started as quickly as possible. This desire can often lead to mistakes and failures. Founders—with their aggressive characteristics—are dedicated to making a successful business despite any interference. They start companies from ground zero, putting in place their own solutions and Vectors. This is how many successful companies have come to be, whether they are Facebook or Amazon.

It is the founder, however, whose strong Vector effect and indomitable spirit can stand in the way of a company's growth. Many founders reach their limits, and their skill set is outstripped by the company's needs. This all-too-natural phenomenon hamstrings many an organization. This same issue is also prevalent with many managers and supervisors who have completed their strategic tasks and start causing damage to the company as it grows bigger and bigger. Their entrepreneurial spirit can make their strong Vector effect extremely negative, decreasing employees' motivation.

CONTROLLING THE VECTOR

As organizations go through a growth cycle, a strong leader should understand that they must withdraw from their previous duties and delegate them to more suitable candidates. They need to trust the staff and the decisions they will make. They also must pick employees who have a strong Vector that won't be affected by others' negative Gravity. This task is not an easy one. Once these employees are chosen, it can lead to growing pains among leadership as new management takes over the helm of the ship. Believe me, I've seen more than one instance of this that puts my teeth on edge.

At EnCata's initial launch, we saw a large number of supervisors and employees come and go. One of these fair-weather staff members gave us an exit interview that changed our thoughts on many of our pressing issues. His head was filled with bright ideas, specifically ones about the Lean manufacturing philosophy. After I caught wind of his proposal, I strongly supported it and put its implementation into motion. Of course, he never had to deal with the lack of activity and narrow-mindedness of his fellow employees. Even he was lazy when it came to the production flow!

Perhaps his laziness—among other reasons—is why he was unable to implement the project into the existing production model. His strength of character allowed me to push him, but his laziness made me push even harder. After a short period, his motivation faded away, and I had to terminate him, despite all my attempts to return him to a usual work routine. Many factors for this situation have converged in this story. Whether it was my endorsement of the employee or his individual mistakes, it doesn't matter. It wasn't even one of the worst things to happen in our company's history.

One of our leading engineers was known not only for his wild passion for work but also his incredible stubbornness. Over the years, we worked with his stubbornness because he helped us design and implement countless solutions. However, it wasn't always easy. Every time he looked at the project I was proposing, he would say it was impossible to implement. Every time, EnCata proved him wrong. This employee was a nonconformist by nature; his opinions were opposed to the CEO's. Eventually, however, he changed his tune. I am proud that today, before he rejects a project, he carefully considers it and tries to get it rolling.

Unfortunately, I was never able to completely change him. By the end of his career at EnCata, all the solutions he had championed were ill fated. His grand ideas became an albatross keeping him from doing the important work he needed to do. In his eyes, however, I looked like a Bluetooth headset, a distinguished despot, glued to the dynamics of the Vector. In the end, I could not put up with his waste of time and came to a few significant conclusions for my sake and that of the company. His dismissal helped create guidelines for how we continue to work with peculiar employees.

DEMANDING PERFORMANCE FROM THE VECTOR

Our current director of the MakeIT Center is an engineer with shining eyes and positive thinking. He is a creative and innovative fellow, dedicated to running our hackerspace. For several years, he was in charge of multiple company projects. He immersed himself in every single one and fell in love with the particulars of each. But his eagerness was not always helpful. His desire to do more added hours to the working day and caused project deadlines to be delayed.

He tried to cope with the workflow, but the assignments snowballed and overtook him. It became obvious to us that he was burned out. One employee couldn't handle over a dozen projects. Personally, I took him off all the tasks and assigned him a much larger project—the MakeIT space. That project eventually became the objective of his professional life. He is in charge of one of the first hackerspaces in the post-Soviet era and assists people who are as much in love with engineering as he is. He is doing what he does best—creating hardware projects. A relatively simple solution allowed me to keep this key employee and give him the opportunity to grow and benefit the company in a different field. But such solutions aren't always so simple. It actually can get much trickier.

In my experience, one of the most difficult employees to deal with is our head of production. An innovative manager, he had the same Vector strength as a founder like me. This crafty employee has the strongest Gravity and Integration as well as the highest loyalty to the company. He never had any weaknesses—except one. He had a tendency to charge ahead, which became his Achilles' heel. While he was a man of established views and morals, he was simply not prepared to face the frequent changes present in the business world. He could not change his Vector—not 18 or 180 degrees.

On the other hand, I kept pushing; I tried really hard to change this person against all odds. It ended the way it was destined to. One day, he came into my office and bitterly suggested that he and the company should part. It was only then that my stubbornness and resentment were fully realized. I knew I needed to change him. I decided to keep him on and used all my passion to make him a more flexible and team-oriented employee. I only did this thanks to the Vector system.

Today, he is a supervisor who is making his first steps that impact his own staff. He, however, has begun to see a situation similar to his own. One of his employees has no Gravity, Integration, or ability to change. This staff member has even been resisting the Vector. While he is still indifferent, this employee has been able to go along with the wind of the company like a sailing yacht—without putting in much effort.

My former employee and his new employee were stuck. Putting up with the pressure, he and his subordinate lost all motivation. They ended up just hanging in there—being neither a boon nor a help to EnCata. In the end, both employees were fired. These experiences we pass on to you, saving you from the resignation letters that you might attract.

VECTORS GONE WRONG

The worst effect of a strong Vector you may come across is large-scale opposition. In the previous chapter, I discussed the Mass Effect phenomenon. In that chapter, I highlighted the interaction of a group of employees with a strong negative Vector and how those can have a negative impact on the company's overall Vector.

It is worth noting that when there is no strong Vector at all, it affects teamwork. Many public institutions lack leaders who devote their entire lives and energy to development. The majority of those who work there are average people, wasting their precious time only to get money in return. Every morning, these work zombies aimlessly go to work only to get the needs to further exist. They do not lead in any way.

The life of a contemporary entrepreneur and CEO is not just an ironed corporate shirt or an expensive Bluetooth headset. It is a nonstop flow of decisions, decisions that change the destiny of the people who feel the strong Vector effect. Coping with this burden on a daily basis is far from being an easy task. That is why a company philosophy and cultural code are necessary to help them avoid obvious business mistakes.

TIPS

1. The strong Vector effect comes from strong-minded entrepreneurs and allows them to create companies and manage a large business. Management and control over this effect is one of the fundamental tasks of a supervisor.

2. During a business growth cycle, founders should withdraw and hand their duties over to more suitable candidates or go through with their decisions by selecting outstanding employees resistant to the strong Vector effect, which is quite difficult at this stage.

3. The worst result of the strong Vector effect is large-scale opposition.

CHAPTER 12

IMAGINARY GRAVITY

Canadians are known for their incredible inventions: peanut butter, garbage bags, cardboard egg trays. Out of all those, however, the most famous Canadian invention is, without a doubt, ice hockey. Even if you do not follow the NHL, you probably know how the game is played. Like many other sports, hockey is about two teams competing. Success depends completely on the collective will to win. This willpower is essential to overcoming the hat tricks, benders, and forechecks. However, it's most noticeable when the team comes together and scores a last-minute game-winning goal.

A formal leader, like a coach or captain, can work as a Gravitator, leading the group to victory. Innately, this person might not have the best team instincts. They might not naturally attract people with their pleasant attitude. They may just be an average guy who's tough, but no better than the rest of his teammates. In fact, he might even be worse—barely able to stand on his skates. He might've barely played a minute in the first period. The player probably has smashed more faces than scored goals in an effort to help his team, convincing them that he needed sensitivity training a long time ago. This player might have just been an addition to round out the numbers.

It's easy to spot these kinds of people in sports. They are visible almost at once. In business, however, it can take months to identify such an example. It is difficult, even when you make it a goal to spot these kinds of situations. Often when a company CEO sees that a department is working well, they will note that the supervisor is acting as a Gravitator, one who deserves the praise *for uniting the team behind a common goal and building their overall gravitational effect.*

This perception, however, might be completely false. The supervisor might not be the Gravitator at all. In fact, it could be one of the employees, an additional supervisor, or even one of the customers that has such a gravitational pull. Their powerful Vector might have sufficient energy to reset the direction and change other Vectors within the team. In this instance, an imaginary Gravity is created, and the team is united under an informal Gravitator—someone who seems unlikely or out of place.

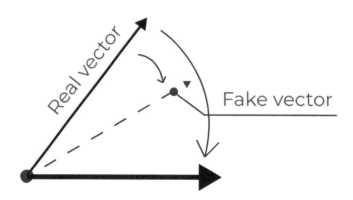

This isn't such a problem when the informal Gravitator has the company's Vector in mind. But letting them go unchecked could cause unforeseen problems. If they aren't working efficiently, production could fall dramatically, causing a complete project shutdown. This is mostly the case when the supervisor, a true team Gravitator, doesn't care enough about their team. The informal Gravitator might even have real leadership skills and claim themselves to be a formal team leader. This can cause a power struggle between the supervisor and the informal Gravitator. This conflict could be bad for business. Nevertheless, it's important that management realizes that a Gravitator can come from anywhere and doesn't need to be formally installed. Over time, a company should identify their true Gravitators.

> IT'S IMPORTANT THAT MANAGEMENT REALIZES THAT A GRAVITATOR CAN COME FROM ANYWHERE AND DOESN'T NEED TO BE FORMALLY INSTALLED. OVER TIME, A COMPANY SHOULD IDENTIFY THEIR TRUE GRAVITATORS.

In most cases, all we need is to know that imaginary Gravity exists along with informal Gravitators. Good managers should rely on it when making up a team. With positive informal and true Gravitators, you have the opportunity to change the Vectors of your team. But if the informal Gravitator has a negative Vector, their Gravity poses a real threat that can't be ignored. If possible, you must cut the impact they have on other Vectors. In case it's negative, the Gravity poses a real threat and is no longer imaginary. You need to cut the impact on the Vectors already affected by this Gravity. The record shows that without positive imaginary Gravity from both supervisors and staff, the team will dissolve. This is especially true if the team supervisor has a weaker gravitational pull.

MONITORING GRAVITY

At the same time, imaginary Gravity is not such a huge problem that requires drastic measures to change. All the supervisor needs to do is limit the team's interaction with the informal Gravitator. That will limit the effect their Gravity has on the team's overall Vector. Most likely, it is better to monitor the **Gravitational Field** of the whole team. From there, you can begin to discern the total Gravity limit, which will give you the total number of employees the informal Gravitator has influence over.

The determined limit of gravitational pull can't be exceeded. Otherwise, the Gravitator will change their direction under the team influence. This situation should be watched closely because imaginary Gravity can have an all-consuming effect. It is impossible to estimate precisely what effort is made to suppress it or coexist with it. A department or the entire company's work efficiency downfall may be a consequence. Therefore, we stand by this principle: *stop hiring new employees if there is no available Gravity to influence and change the team.*

Over the years, we often encountered this idea of imaginary Gravity on our teams. This is often highly dependent on the makeup of the team, including the customers and the supervisors. While running one of our projects, the team showed incredible results, thanks to the high Gravity within and thanks to a large investment of my own time in the work. Once they were off and running, I left them to their own devices and failed to keep in touch for some time.

Unfortunately, the formal leader couldn't prevent the team breakup and dissolution of Gravity. The project appeared close to shutdown and required my urgent intervention. I spent time getting internal connections to help reset the project to its initial Vector path. Today, I have regular interaction with the team's formal Gravitator. Despite all this, however, it has not been beneficial for the project. Dealing with Gravity is a long process, and there is no guarantee it will end successfully.

Moreover, we took a number of measures to change things within the team. We appointed a long-term supervisor to take over the project. This individual had worked on several projects throughout the company and was seen as a true Gravitator. Within a few months, however, it was clear that his Gravity was insufficient, and the team fell apart once again. We kept transferring employees in and out of the team. I tried to influence the supervisor individually, but none of these tactics brought success. We had to break them up and start the whole department from scratch. We appointed new managers and monitored the **Gravitational Field** of the team. It was only this way that we could solve such a hidden and insidious issue as imaginary Gravity. That's why every time your team hits the ice, support your favorite striker, captain, and coach—even that plain-looking guy with missing teeth who shows up in the arena and smiles all the time.

TIPS

1. Imaginary Gravity is the informal Gravitator's impact on the team.

2. Quite often one of the employees, a supervisor, or a customer may be a Gravitator.

3. Without a Gravitator, the work efficiency of the team will fall.

4. A true Gravitator within the team is not always a leader.

CHAPTER 13

CHEMISTRY AND TEAM BUILDING

In the past few years, I have hardly ever left my seat when I am in an airplane. Was I feeling comfortable? Of course. Did I enjoy the mode of transportation? Not really. In fact, flying would probably rank up there as one of my least favorite ways to travel. I know without a doubt that it is safe, comfortable, and fast, but for me it is just a means of getting to a destination. Train travel, however, is a completely different experience. A long trip in a spacious train compartment can bring true joy to a passenger.

Breathtaking views from the window, light vibration from the window glass, and interesting conversationalists can turn each trip into an exciting adventure. Traveling by train around Belarus and its neighbors is a unique experience. Not every train is pleasing to the eye, and some passengers keep silent. Baked chicken is served in the foil it was cooked in and has the ability to destroy your sense of smell, and maybe even the distressed linen on your foldout bed. Despite all this, however, the jolting train is not the worst option. These dangerous meals and dirty sheets are a distinctive feature of a railway trip in this part of the world.

But sometimes, your expectations fail you, and your neighbor is captivating and charismatic. You find yourself talking to them with ease. This person, who might not have captured your attention on the street, is the most beautiful person to you. Someone who was silent a few minutes ago opens up and shines in new splendor. A passing connection forms between the two of you without any pressure. Spending a long time in a confined space has opened you up to talking. The shared journey gave you a conversation starter. In an open space, we often dream of meeting many people—idols and cult leaders. After a while, however, you'll find these conversationalists are boring out in the wild when compared to your train buddy.

> CHEMISTRY IS INSEPARABLE FROM GRAVITY. **IT IS THE MENTAL CLOSENESS OF ONE PERSON TO ANOTHER AT A CERTAIN MOMENT.**

This doesn't mean that the person on the train is more educated, more well mannered, or better looking than your average person. It means that you established a mental connection with that person. This is called **chemistry**. Chemistry is inseparable from Gravity. It is the mental closeness of one person to another at a certain moment. A person's chemistry is revealed upon their first meeting. It allows them to start friendly talks on board the train that can lead to hiring suitable candidates. Chemistry between people is like a tunnel in physics, which increases Integration and Gravity between people

Please note that "chemistry" and "Gravity" are used not as scientific definitions here. We have assigned these terms our own meaning.

Supervisors with a powerful chemistry bond between themselves and most of the employees will be successful in making their people work. And not just their own folks, but employees in other departments as well, especially when it comes to short-term tasks. After a number of successful joint projects, other employees will come to admire that particular department, headed by that supervisor. As a result, a self-building team is formed around the Gravitator and Integrator with the same strong chemistry.

Such teams are made naturally. We had a good example of a team of payroll officers with a strong Gravitator, but with a weak Integrator in charge. The supervisor had built this team naturally through chemistry and Gravity. However, he sometimes failed in achieving goals set by the department. These goals were specifically about regular communications with his subordinates. If the supervisor was both Integrator and Gravitator, he would have managed to bring the employees together on his own. In this case, we had to force the employees to communicate. Unnatural teams are built around a particular Gravitator or Integrator who is appointed by senior managers. Such teams have to be built due to the business needs and the hierarchical management system that exists in many companies.

EVOLVING SELF-PROPELLED TEAMS

A team can be built without any Integrator or Gravitator. Such self-building teams are based around the projects the employee chooses. People gather around a problem to solve it. This same work methodology gave us the most iconic computer games: Warcraft and Half-Life 2. During the operation, employees can randomly build teams for a specific project. This behavior is highly encouraged by management. Each and every desk has small wheels to move around the office, so employees can be like a mobile unit, taking down problems no matter where they are. If an employee is into a particular project, they just "roll up" to the team involved. If the team approves, the new employee joins and starts working. At any time, that individual can "roll away" from the team, especially if they think their contribution is done or they're no longer a good fit for the project.

We also try to implement such elements in the work of our teams. Even with such rapid cooperation, the team makes an independent cell. It can transition to a certain ecosystem and make it possible for a few employees performing similar tasks to bring a creative nuance to their project. One of the key team members will eventually emerge as a stronger Gravitator and become an informal or formal team leader.

Employees who roll up to new projects are more willing to work and better themselves. They raise their intelligence level at an incredible pace by developing their Gravity. Management might take notice and appoint them to bigger positions. Numerous studies show that the average intelligence level of a supervisor is higher than that of his or her subordinates. This doesn't prove, however, that people with higher intelligence get managerial positions. These new positions are only achieved if an employee stretches their mind and learns to solve problems like a supervisor.

THE CONDUCIVE WORK CULTURE

Group dynamics is a large issue that we do not have space to get into in this book. Suffice it to say that environment and order are two huge contributing factors when people gather to build a team. A company might have an ideal environment for building teams, such as an open-concept floor plan or mobile workstations, but without the order—the rules for how and why you can group with others—the environment is meaningless.

Thanks to the educational systems established in the nineteenth century, we live in a world governed by a collection of standards and rules. In the past hundred years, the world has welcomed an avalanche of inventions and a number of technological revolutions. These days it is very important to consolidate standards in business processes to get a comprehensive flow that yields top results. When a company has to make sustainable structural changes, they should be based on standards that will be more effective than natural environmental improvement. The work order should support the flawless work environment in proper conditions while working toward overarching objectives.

No matter how important the order is, an environment can overcome the carefully placed set of standards. If an employee is not structurally connected with the company's workspace, the task of the business is to create the most comfortable conditions for employees' maximum production. This is especially true if your employee performs a complex creative task. An easy way to reward an employee for creating a cultural code might be handing them a cool daiquiri and a one-way ticket to the nearest warm coast. I'm kidding, of course! Move the drink cooler closer to their chair.

ASSESSMENT OF WORK CANDIDATES

The basic personality traits of each employee are one of the important factors in creating an effective team. Their inborn features, nurtured in the home environment and their prior education experiences, are key contributors to their present performance. These innate characteristics are difficult to change. A recruiter must assess a candidate or current employee's past training and culture while passing judgment on them as future employees. If all the physics talk in the past few chapters has been tiring, that's fine. We'll use agriculture as our next metaphor.

Every year when you cultivate land and plant rye, you harvest about a hundred tons of rye per hectare (2.4 acres). As soon as you stop cultivating the land, you will harvest only twenty kilos of rye in the first year. In the second year, you'll harvest only ten kilos. In the third year, your field will be completely covered with weeds. Agriculturalists, however, found the best solution to this problem. The main control method is selective farming. In this style of farming, you select cultures (strains of different work projects) that complement each other and grow in harmony—instead of working with the weeds of your department.

In this same way, self-built teams are subject to imbalance and destabilization without proper control from management. Only by selecting cultures and experimenting with new standards in the working life of the team is it possible to build a balanced team with the right chemistry, Integration, and Gravity surrounded by an ideal environment.

TIPS

1. Chemistry is inseparable from Gravity. It shows the mental closeness of one person to another at a certain moment.

2. A natural self-building team is formed around a Gravitator and Integrator with the same chemistry.

3. Unnatural teams are also built organically, but ultimately, they should be focused around a particular Gravitator or Integrator.

4. On the whole, a team can be built without any Integrator or Gravitator. Sooner or later a team player will emerge as a Gravitator or an Integrator.

5. Usually the average intelligence level of a supervisor is higher than that of his or her subordinates. The employees under them might become supervisors only if they stretch their minds and learns to make decisions under different circumstances.

6. Self-building teams' activity is influenced by environment, order, basic features of each particular employee, and maturity of HR processes in the company.

CHAPTER 14

NATURAL VECTOR ANGLE CHANGE

Each parent is directly responsible for bringing up their child. Every day, parents invest energy, money, and time in creating the best version of ourselves through their children. As a parent myself, I am all too aware of this situation. We anxiously track the progress of our offspring by checking their homework. We educate them through long conversations, where we share our own morality, ethics, and aesthetics. We believe in socialization, as do many other parents. At the first opportunity, we give the child to an educational institution—the place where they will receive the necessary knowledge. There they learn the sciences and humanities, but they also get their first lessons in modern society.

No matter how hard we try, however, this process does not always result in a fully formed person who is in harmony with the world around them. Society is chaotic, and the educational process doesn't always result in a logical conclusion. Unfortunate and unforeseen things happen that can affect how our children grow into adults. Illnesses, deaths, and divorces cannot be expected and therefore cannot be planned for. Divorce in developed countries is steadily approaching or exceeding 50 percent of the total number of marriages. This could be viewed as the starting point for the decline of moral principles and the erosion of the foundations of our children's morality. A child left without a parent—or worse, without any guardians—will face many problems in their future. Divorce and our diminishing morality have created a hole in the bulwark of our society. Without the daily influence of a strong familial leader, our children's sense of ethics will gradually fade into the background, and mercantile goals become the main purpose of existence. It has been statistically proven that the majority of criminals or people with mental disorders come from single-parent families.

The tasks of a modern socially responsible business are similar to those embraced by the traditional family unit. Every day the head of the company influences employees. Their behavior should be an example for everyone below them—a good CEO leads by example. Their closest managers are agents of corporate philosophy. Ordinary employees must feel the attention and care for themselves in the existing corporate paradigm. This caring should not only be based building the skills of the employees but their moral qualities as well. Just as the family unit needs every member in order to succeed, every employee is responsible for the well-being of the company. This well-being is primary. It is just as important during slow seasons as it is during busy ones. The people we surround ourselves with in the office must be like a second family that requires nurturing and care.

No one knows, however, when tragedy will strike. In the case of force majeure, we postpone all our employees' tasks and help those affected to find ways out. We do this even in the most unpleasant situations. While the global Gravitational Field of our company was artificially created by our founders, it is not immune to the behaviors and emotions of our staff. Problems in the personal life of a single employee could affect how an entire team operates. And that team's new behavior could impact the whole company. Furthermore, employees are comforted when the company takes an active role in helping solve problems that don't relate to the workplace. This encourages employee well-being and belief in the company.

THE DANGER OF MANAGERIAL WITHDRAWAL

As soon as a supervisor decides to withdraw from management, they leave this second family incomplete. Their influence over employees will wane, and the staff will feel the effects immediately. When you stop practicing corporate philosophy, you are effectively destroying the company's global Gravitational Field. After some time, employee Vectors revert to their previous state—years of advancement and cohesion may be wasted.

In this situation, employees are like metal. While under a good manager, they will feel the pull of their magnetic field. Deprived of this energy, however, those retained magnetic properties will fade, and they will go back to their initial state. If the influence of a magnetic field is constant over a long period of time, the metal itself becomes a magnet and may be strong enough to resist reverting to its previous state. Therefore, long-term impact on the employee's Vector is a priority goal for the company. After all, the longer a strong Gravitational Field is absent, the higher the probability of loss not for individual employees, but for the company as a whole. The entire corporate system gradually collapses from the point of view of a general under-standing of corporate philosophy.

DON'T RECEDE—
ALWAYS GO FORWARD!

It is worth noting that an employee, even if they are ignored and uncared for by a company, will not change their outlook on the world when this happens. Their ethical position will only roll back to the level that was formed earlier. They will return to their own equilibrium, a state of stable balance. This negative reverse movement is also possible at this stage. It is only necessary to overcome new inertia. However, the new balanced state of the employee might already have been affected by your strong corporate philosophy.

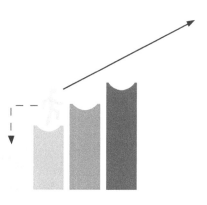

Everything in the physical world seeks to achieve a state of equilibrium. This principle is also a necessary premise in business and is especially evident when an employee climbs the ranks in your company.

Passing through each barrier, climbing a step higher, an employee can become an indivisible part of the company under the influence of corporate philosophy. The employee's understanding of the world is changing in the necessary direction, and the Angle of their Vector becomes closer and closer to that of the company. The higher an employee climbs up the ladder, the easier it will be to return them to the state of stable equilibrium from the previous stage. If there is no global Gravitational Field, they will fall only one step back to their previous energy state.

UPWARD MOBILITY

In order to transfer an employee to another level, a manager needs to spend manpower and energy. The task of the leader is to constantly work on the development of their people and to ensure the transition of energy to get them to the next step. Over the years, the process of continuous improvement has become the main principle of our company. We track the development of each employee. Any stop or wavering in their career trajectory means regression to us. Any and all employee development is our joint achievement.

To ensure a full development that helps the entire company, we at EnCata monitor and influence a number of factors that constantly affect the energy state of an employee:

SALARY

We believe all work should be paid with dignity. Despite the fact that the level of wages corresponds to market indicators, we do not ignore the expectations of the employees themselves. The company has a bonus system for initiatives and standards. Several times a year, a salary review is conducted on the basis of monthly KPIs, or key performance indicators. In individual cases, we also provide one-time financial assistance to employees in need. This is part of our corporate philosophy of caring for our employees.

TEAM

Team building is a long process that requires massive numbers of man-hours. Each team should be built around appropriate skills but also similar Vectors. At EnCata, we've used our team-building experience to research team dynamics and interpersonal relationships. Based on that research, we've created our own teams. It's up to you to figure out the dynamics and Vectors of your own company and how that affects the creation of teams.

PLACE IN A TEAM

Every employee should be comfortable in their team. Even a small contribution to the common cause creates goodwill and enthusiasm. Each employee needs to understand in their own way how they are contributing to the results of the team. Understanding the value of their activities is what makes an employee loyal to the company.

GUIDE

Each manager in the company has passed all stages of company indoctrination and understands the structures of all job descriptions below and above their position. The task of the company is to select a leader who not only matches the skills and Vectors of his or her team but sets an example of leadership for the team. Not all employees are willing to accept an authoritarian leader immediately. Democratic leadership also has its issues when urgent and important tasks need to be done quickly. If all employees are on the same Vector, it's easy to make rapid decisions in a democratic company. This often happens in a nonprofit organization where a team is ideologically driven.

SOCIALIZATION PROCESSES

The need for constant communication among staff is smoothed out when social events are held. We do not like noisy and massive corporate events. These are often a waste of company funds and manpower. In addition, bringing together teams of differing Vectors could lead to unpredictable consequences. We've found that the best way is to hold small events in the team—for example, organizing a movie night exclusively in a foreign language for department employees who use this language in their everyday work. In order to ensure positive communication between departments, we organize these events during down times and ensure that positive interactions are held. Some of the most popular events at EnCata revolve around sports and eSports games. A little healthy competition in the form of football or table tennis tournaments helps keep spirits up during the stress of a workweek.

COMPANY STATUS

Google and Apple employees are often well known in their field because they work for such prestigious companies. They do not need additional motivation. They believe that the future of the whole world depends on them. Crafting the image of a company is a long-term task that can't always be measured in numbers and results. If a modern company, however, brushes aside the promotion of their own brand, it can only lead to a dire failure of the organization. Only a successful, efficient, and stable business that has a positive reputation will attract the best employees in the labor market.

FAMILY

Family is a special topic for many employees who devote their lives to work. We are hypersensitive to relationships on our teams and attempt to monitor them when appropriate. The company also checks in on changes in the psychological state of employees and tries to assist in solving personal problems. We realize this is a slippery slope in America, but if handled correctly, it can do wonders for the employee—both at home and in the workplace.

This important list of conditions stated above constantly affect the natural change in the Angle of a Vector. Given the vast number of variables, it's impossible for every business to directly influence each of these points. The formation of loyalty is an invisible process—

sometimes even to the trained eye. A mistake in that delicate process that can lead to a halt in the relationship between the company and the employee. It's obvious that this is a catastrophic result. This error could become a setback for corporate philosophy overall. Therefore, it is necessary for every CEO, every HR manager, and anyone in a leadership position to remember that the employer's direct duty is to educate everyone within their sphere of influence.

TIPS

1. The global Gravitational Field of the company creates a continuous forward momentum that affects both employees' skills and their morality.

2. Tasks not related to work activity that are successfully solved by the company maximize that employee's loyalty.

3. When you let your corporate philosophy become stagnant, you remove the global Gravitational Field of the company.

4. The longer a strong Gravitational Field is absent in an employee's day-to-day work, the higher the probability of loss of that individual employee. This leads to a loss for the company, as the entire corporate system gradually collapses.

5. The process of continuous improvement is the basic principle of a modern company. It is necessary to track the development of each employee. Any stoppage in their development is regression and degradation.

6. To ensure harmonious development, it is necessary to monitor and influence a number of factors that constantly affect the energy state of an employee.

CHAPTER 15

CHANGING THE VECTOR'S DIRECTION

Most of the world's business organizations, from Amazon to a coffee shop in Mongolia, have had their operations disrupted with dire consequences during 2020. The survival of tens of thousands of organizations will be determined by a rapid pivot to a new Vector Angle set forth by the Gravitators and disseminated to the employees by the Integrators. "Nonessential" businesses must move quickly to cut costs and align themselves with "essential" providers. If this is not feasible, companies must quickly assess their marketplace and make rapid, often dramatic changes to ensure their survival. It is estimated that up to 30 percent of businesses worldwide will suffer dire financial consequences of the pandemic. Firms must "en masse" change their strategy and direction driven by a rapidly adapting Vector.

There is a method of changing Vectors—a whole system of events aimed at the long-term results for each employee. During the proper implementation of this system, employees within an organization grow into hardworking professionals that represent the loyal ideology of the idea of the business. Given the current trends in the labor market, however, this is a difficult pursuit. Modern employees want to be independent from a company and treated as a partner rather than a subordinate. In order to do so, they demonstrate their value through their day-to-day activities.

Being a partner, however, comes with risks to both parties. Employees don't understand that this partnership could hurt them should they falter or stray from the company Vector. This is especially true in the case of low-quality-of-service providers who have a high rate of turnover. This lack of honesty about positioning creates an imbalance that can hurt both employee and organization. Companies should avoid such candidates for employment on principle. They should find less experienced but more flexible workers who will grow with the company.

We pay separate attention to the preliminary stages of an employee's Vector changes. In order to make the correct decision, we analyze the data collected by monitoring an employee's first several months with EnCata. This process includes the following:

1. A survey and interview

On a monthly basis, management should survey the leaders and the staff on their feedback and proposals to improve the overall output of the company. Surveying is a good method for collecting this common data, and it allows management to make decisions based on the will of their employees. For example, by conducting such surveys, management can determine the most comfortable time to begin the workday for the team. Moreover, these polls are conducted monthly and are supported by individual discussions held between team leaders and their employees. These conversations are usually held during review time and are measured against the KPIs of the employee.

2. Observation and analysis of the behavior of employees

This method is a must for the leaders of teams. Observation is the process that is permanently on the work activity agenda. Analysis must be done at least once a month. In the course of data analysis, a leader evaluates the following parameters of an employee on a scale of 0 to 100:

- A show of solidarity and support of their colleagues

- A sense of freedom and independence

- Overall satisfaction with the result of the employee's work

- A tendency to follow orders from supervisors and management

- Management tendencies

- How freely an employee expresses his or her opinions as well as feelings and desires

- The ability of the employee to orient, to inform, to explain, and to advise

- The interest in the evaluation of the employee's own actions

- How the employee gives out instructions and explains methods of work to others

- The level of disagreement, sabotage, or failure to help colleague's formalism in action

- Evasion of joint action

- Manifestation of annoyance, aggression, belittlement of other colleagues' merits, inadequate assessment of employees' role on the team

3. Conversation with employees

At the end of each month, management should have full and thorough conversations with each employee on their KPIs. In these meetings, team leaders should cover work tasks, evaluation of growth areas, and goals and desires of the employee. In addition, the team leader must find out certain personal information about the employee and their attitude toward their work. Questions for the employee must be extremely short and pursue a specific target:

- Find out the level of satisfaction of the employee's own actions and work.

- Find out the level of satisfaction of the team leader as well as the company in general.

4. The study results

After this monthly check-in, team leaders will have certain information that is necessary to structure their future management style. These managers must create a table for their employees, where each person's data will be displayed on the Vector path. They will be rated on a scale of 0 to 100 in the following parameters:

- **Skill level**: This is defined based on the evaluation of the tasks completed by an employee.

- **Gravity level:** This is determined during the first year of work. It will usually remain constant throughout their entire time of employment.

- **Integration level:** This will also be determined during the first year of work. Just like Gravity, it usually remains constant throughout the employee's career.

- **Loyalty level:** This is defined by data gathered through observation, analysis, and personal interviews with the employee.

- **Property to change:** This is the level that illustrates how much an employee's tasks change throughout the first couple of months in the organization.

- **The rate of change:** This is determined by how punctual an employee is when finishing work based on a deadline.

The Vector of the team leader must be rated by a higher-level manager. For CEOs and their HR directors, it is necessary that they take into account the additional criteria. These evaluations should consider certain Vectors in order to accurately judge the team leader:

- **Group expectations:** This is the analysis of the staff and their perception of the leader, as well as other department heads and leaders.

- **Assessment of the group norm:** A status quo of the team leader's staff. This is an implementation as well as analysis of the team at its current level of leadership.

- **Employee growth:** How does the team leader implement the interests of the team as a whole and use those to grow individual employees?

- **Loyalty to the company:** The team leader's level of commitment to the ideals of the business and their potential to be spread within a team. It is important here to distinguish between loyalty and conformity. Conformed leaders carry a number of potential threats to corporate philosophy. Loyal leaders create an atmosphere for the implementation of the most incredible projects.

- **Gravity:** Gravitators are always in short supply. The leader with natural Gravity is a valuable element of corporate philosophy and is a valuable tool to change the Vector of employees.

- **Integration:** An assessment of the possibility of the team leader to promote teamwork to resolve tasks. This also includes an evaluation of the performance level of the leader through interaction and communication in the team.

- **Leadership:** This is a classification of the team leader's leadership skills (situational, universal, etc.), personality (inspirational leadership), and the style of leadership (authoritarian or democratic).

- **Conduct of work-free-time activities:** This ranks how a team leader is utilizing "work-free" time and if it is being used for training, corporate events, or socializing.

After this analysis, data managers can show the Vector of team leaders for additional visualization of the current situation in the team. If alterations in the Vector are necessary, a subordinate leader or higher manager should employ the following methodologies:

1. Gravity

If the leader is falling behind, their team should be introduced to an additional gravitational source. The impact of strong Gravitators with corporate vision will help set the direction of the Vector from the outside. The founder of the company could become such an external factor. It is often the founder who is the most powerful Gravitator and has the maximum true Vector. Such an energized executive is gifted with the incredible ability to unite people. Their time is usually very limited and consumes incredible amounts of cash flow for the company.

2. Natural

This method is effective when it is necessary to manage a smaller number of employees. Usually, that number is somewhere under ten. It is then that the Gravitator will have an immediate impact on their subordinates. It is necessary for team leaders to allocate more of their time to interact with specific employees in order to change their Vector. The addition of a new leader who has high Gravity can correctly direct the Vector of employees, even if those employees have already changed a number of departments in the company.

3. Method Sectors

In the first stages of a team's formation, the group is often multi-Vectored—a kind of mix of professions, ideology, and motivation. In these cases, it can be difficult to determine the Vector. In order to regulate each Vector, groups can be divided into sectors where each person has a Gravitator whose Vector is closest to the Vector of the employees. In cases like this, Disintegrators must be eliminated from the team completely. Over time, these sectors must be gradually combined in order to form a successful team. For example, during the formation period of our marketing team, a Disintegrator was excluded, and a multi-Vectoral team was divided into subsectors. By forming separate areas of responsibility for Integrators, each department contributed to the improvement of employee loyalty. This allowed them to come together as a whole and benefit the mother ship.

Systems involve the subjective selection and combination of methods on the basis of the collected and analyzed data during the early stages of a company's development. The use of the above methods will help leaders not only improve the loyalty of employees but also increase the skills of each individual employee.

TIPS

1. In order to change Vectors, systems of measures must be created with the goal of creating long-term results for each employee.

2. Monitoring is the most important part of these systems. It includes a survey and interview, monitoring and analysis of the employee's behavior, a conversation with an employee, and a study of the employee's productivity.

3. If the impact on the Vector of a subordinate leader or higher manager is necessary, resort to the following methods: gravitational, natural, and method sectors.

4. This system involves the subjective selection and combination of the methods on the basis of the collected and analyzed data during the prestages.

CHAPTER 16

THE VECTOR FUNNEL

"We need to talk." Upon hearing this phrase, most people will begin to tremble. The uncertainty of this "talk" frightens most everyone. No one knows how it will end. Imagine, for instance, you're a married couple. You have the talk, and afterward, you file for divorce. Today, you could be a candidate in a job interview, but tomorrow, after that talk, you could be an employee—even a manager. Almost anything is possible after a talk.

In the last couple of years, we have led hundreds of talks at EnCata. These have been in the form of interviews or discussions primarily around the concept of role-playing. Through the concept of role playing, we've examined and analyzed our hiring process. From the most minute detail to the biggest-picture problems, we've gone over absolutely everything that can be covered in the hiring and onboarding process. Based on our research, we have created a preliminary method of hiring employees based on empirical data.

This data helped us create the **Funnel of Vectors** theory we have discussed previously. This Funnel allows management to select exactly those who fit the company and its objectives at that exact right moment. This Funnel allows organizations to hit that moving target right after the first live interview. In the years of the Soviet Union, there was a popular phrase coined by the dictator Joseph Stalin: "Human resources solve all." Around the same time, a famous American management consultant remarked, "The right process gives the right results." At EnCata, we have combined these sayings into our own guiding principle: the correct processes are only done by the correct people. This is, in a nutshell, the theory that guides the creation of the Funnel. Each HR manager must understand the best way to create their own Funnel of Vectors. These managers must use only a couple of interviews to evaluate the Vector of the candidate against the Vector of the company. This process is illustrated below:

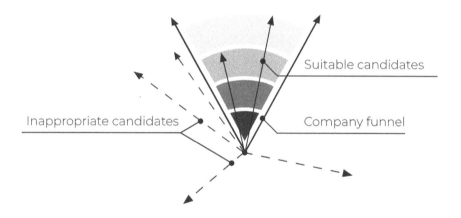

A Funnel of Vectors allows for an acceptable deviation of the candidate from the company Vector based on moral, ethical, and philosophical principles. The first conversation in an interview should be as simple as comparing your basic moral foundation with that of the potential hire. Already within this talk, you will find where the candidate falls in your Funnel. For example, let's say you were opening a casino. It would go against your ethical principles to hire a recovering gambling addict. Instead, pick employees who would do well working in an environment that includes gambling. These kinds of people will not let you down.

Candidates with the right moral background have been through multiple stages of our selection process. These initial conversations do not usually go beyond discussing moral and ethical principles. When we see that there is no radical conflict between management and a potential employee, we move on to the next phase of interviews.

Despite our best attempts, however, it's possible that an HR manager might be incapable of calculating the Vector of a candidate in this first interview. There are several reasons for this. One of them might be simple nepotism. It might be shocking, but having a good conversation with a potential coworker might not be the most relaxing interaction. It's even more tense when the person who works next to you is that candidate's good friend or partner. This nepotistic hiring practice might seem easy for everyone, but it could harm the company's overall Vector.

Furthermore, candidates who express excessive loyalty to the company in the first interview should not always be trusted. They might not be a good fit for the overall Vector. Their extra "commitment" can conceal mercenary intentions. A hiring manager, however, should never despair. One fine day, a candidate might walk into your office with a slovenly disposition yet has perfect speech, exceptional skills, and a readiness to change. After the interview, the HR supervisor and the direct manager will claim that this candidate is "our candidate."

You must be certain, though, before you offer the chance to go through a test day and eventually the test month. During that trial period, observation of the employee can assist in developing an opinion about them and their work. And it isn't just the HR manager's job to observe but that of all the stakeholders involved in the hiring process. These are crucially important steps that reveal additional variables in the employee's Vector, such as skills, loyalty, Gravity, Integration, and ability to change the speed of the Vector.

Even if you are completely pleased with the moral principles of the new employee, that doesn't guarantee they'll be a diligent worker. It's even possible that on their first test day, the employee will go out for lunch and never come back. While this might leave you shocked, unnerved, and frankly upset, let's forget about those things for now. Time is the most precious resource that you have, and you use a lot of it in the course of selecting future employees. Remember that the length of the Vector (skills) can always be changed by applying minor adjustments. In-company training sessions and courses in an employee's field and additional education within the company can often solve the problem of unskilled labor. The most difficult task in hiring new staff is not determining the length of their Vector, but the Angle of it—how the company fits into their own goals and visions.

SPIRITUAL ALIGNMENT

This is why, in the first interview, we ask ourselves, "Who is this person exactly?" Only after hiring do we ponder, "What are they capable of achieving?" Our years of research have shown that if a person is close in spirit with the company, it's easy to grow them into a team professional with the appropriate skills and experience. It is much more difficult to find a "ready" professional and adapt them to your company's culture. It's not always possible or even likely that you'll meet a specialist in exactly the shape you need to bring them on as an employee. On one occasion, we almost let one young engineer go, until we found out that he had an unsurpassed talent in the creation of video content. Today he is a key employee in the marketing department. He found his space at EnCata because we trusted his Vector.

We often hire younger folks at EnCata because we're passionate about watching them grow with us. These strong-willed newcomers stick to their positions, and with time, their Vector begins to align with that of the founder. They begin to feel a sense of ownership and pride for the company. However, it takes work from the company as well. From the first moment these future professionals, idols of youth, come to us, we must constantly steer them into the proper channels. In time, they begin to realize that they've been working in a specific environment and have grown into specialists. Often, they're amazed at how their skills surpass those of their respective peers.

Despite our tendency to hire younger, there are still those enticing "ready to hire" candidates with the skills necessary for a certain project. These candidates are usually motivated only by a desire to make money—sometimes to a fault. But never fear! A hiring manager should not hesitate to hire these kinds of employees, especially for a young company or division. They might even tell you right away that they are doing your company a favor. Don't let their precocious attitude deter you, however! Make sure to include them in projects outside of work and social events so they feel like they are part of the team. Even nonmaterial motivations such as a healthy working atmosphere can boost the loyalty of even the greediest employee.

Nowadays, we have stopped spending resources on such money-driven candidates and self-appointed rock stars of commerce. The Funnel of our company has changed radically in the last few years. The flexibility of the Funnel allows the corporate HR process to adapt to the changes of the contemporary labor market. We either take in the anomalies of specific instances or reject them from our research. This is how the Funnel may change its size and position. This is especially true in the case of a change of a Vector of the company or forced rapid growth.

As a company grows, the requirements toward candidates change and evolve. In spite of this growth in size and staff, it is the task of the CEO and HR department to constantly decrease the size of the

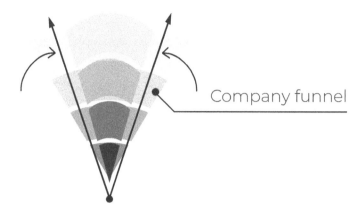

Company funnel

Vector Funnel and to decrease the Angle of the Vector at different stages of employee selection. By doing so, they will see an increase of the effectiveness of the company and within the HR department itself. Not only does this increase the amount of correctly Vectored workers, but it also hones the Vector of the employees more to the Vector of the business.

RAPID GROWTH AND STRAIN ON THE SYSTEM

If the company expands incredibly quickly or deviates its direction, hiring managers should go back to the old system of hiring with a larger Vector Funnel. This retroactive methodology allows the expansion of human resources quicker so they can solve the difficulties of a sudden spurt in growth. This expanded Funnel, however, shouldn't be allowed to go on forever. The timeframe of the expanded Funnel must be limited and controlled by external forces such as the CEO and head of HR. By expanding your Vector Funnel, you introduce a variety of new Vectors into your system. The interaction of all these different Vectors can lead to chaotic consequences. In addition, this retroactive process can erode the general loyalty of the team and further inflame management paralysis. This will set off a series of events that are irreversible and can cripple or destroy the team.

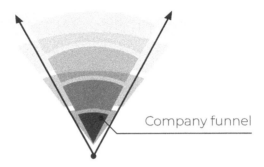

Company funnel

The change of the location of the Funnel is also a natural movement in the HR process. This will usually happen right after a change of the direction of the business. Pivots into new directions for the business require new workers with differing levels of skills and even different basic principles. In that scenario, the Funnel can shift tens of degrees, and formerly loyal employees can become displeased and unaccepting of the new directives from leadership.

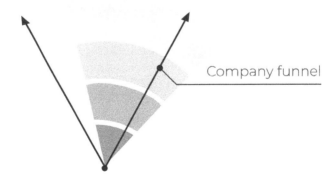

Company funnel

By expanding and contracting our Vector Funnel, we helped solve staffing problems, one key worker at a time. During the preliminary open Funnel phase, we were confident that the Vector of the workers we needed would fit into the existing Funnel. However, there was one financial worker who surprised us. We did everything to change him in a better direction and tie him to the business while giving the opportunity to grow with us. Over the course of five years, the Vector of this employee did not change. We tried surrounding him with active workers and strong Gravitators, but his Vector did not budge. Eventually, we had to say goodbye to this employee. During that five-year period, not only did the company begin to actively expand in its size, but we also changed the direction of the business. This meant that the Funnel narrowed and shifted. The Vector of this employee remained immovable.

Almost immediately it became clear that this employee's actions were beginning to have a negative impact on the well-being of the corporation. We soon had to terminate this toxic relationship. We value loyalty above all else, but we're also able to adapt to support specific employees. Even in the most complicated situations, we find the solution to retain valuable personnel.

THE VECTOR IS LIKE A TORNADO

Apart from the existing Funnel in the company and its tendency to change, it is important to remember that the Vector's size and position will always be limited by the general Gravitational Field. The task of creating such a Gravitational Field is an artificial process that is another goal of the HR department, as well as of management and the founder. The Gravitational Field is like a collection of magnets that attract prospective employees. These magnets are things like financial compensation, corporate philosophy, and unique colleagues. If you withdraw that energy of magnetic attraction, then the system will go into a self-controlling mode. Each department will form separate cultures that will conflict with each other. In that case, the formal presence of a Gravitational Field will unite each employee with a common vision. Once that is installed, there will be harmony again, and a renewed momentum toward growth.

TIPS

1. A Funnel of Vectors is the collective movement of the company. It shows an acceptable deviation between the Vector of the candidate and that of the company.

2. The HR department, along with management and the founder, creates this Funnel and bases its flexibility on the moral and ethical principles of the company.

3. When first encountering a candidate, it is enough to compare your basic organizational norms and values with those of the potential employee in order to see if they fit within your Vector Funnel.

4. Hiring managers should be wary of candidates who are excessively loyal. It is important to differentiate loyalty from initial chemistry, which can fade within the first month. As a result, the job seeker who seemed the most gung ho may end up being the wrong fit for the company.

5. The Funnel can change its size and location. In changing its size, it is important to take into account the possible consequences for the employees bound to the change of the Vector's new direction.

6. The size and the location of the Funnel are limited by the general Gravitational Field and the current direction of the Vector of the company.

7. The Gravitational Field is the collective magnetic energy of the organization and how it affects prospective candidates and holds current employees in the correct position.

8. When the Gravitational Field is "withdrawn," the system will go into the self-controlling mode, and separate cultures of each division of the company will form, which will likely create drastic consequences.

CHAPTER 17

MAINTAINING THE TEAM VECTOR

Sometimes, due to circumstances outside their control, an employee with very little experience will be elevated to manager of a large team. Often, they're unable to wield such a large group on their first attempt at management, and they're forever marred as "not management material." The most successful managers learn by taking over small teams and understanding how their work leading those teams impacts the larger company. In this chapter, we will show you how a whole company works by illustrating the processes of formation, interaction, and development of a smaller teams. Teams are the beginning of a unit—the practical application of the theory of Vectors.

As an example, let's look at the software development department at EnCata. This team consists of thirty-five employees with presumably a multiple variety of Vectors and various levels of loyalty. The task is to change the Angle of the team's Vector and guide each employee in the direction of the company's Vector. The implementation of such a task is assigned to the leader. The leader then begins to work on the formation of collective Vectors with a detailed table that depicts the current state of their subordinates. Managers should update such a tracking document at least once a month.

	Name	Skills	Loyalty	Gravity	Integration	Flexibility	Rate of change	Chemistry
1	Hines T.	44	60	21	21	YES	55	
2	Terry M.	17	30	48	38	YES	68	
3	Baker M.	51	30	91	80	YES	30	
4	Sims A.	87	-15	67	67	NO	-	
5	Norton L.	54	0	20	20	NO	-	
6	Preston T.	31	45	14	25	YES	78	
7	Beasley B.	28	30	15	15	YES	10	
...	Wiggins L.	76	-5	13	20	YES	35	
33	O'Brien A.	88	0	53	53	NO	-	
34	Booker D.	47	75	67	67	YES	55	
35	Ross P.	72	90	25	40	YES	64	

The first column is for the names of employees. A leader is obliged to include absolutely all of the workers on their list—including those who are still in their testing and training period.

Skills
44
17
51
87
54
31
28
76
88
47
72

The second column is dedicated to training staff—the length of the Vector. It is impossible to assess the brightness or dullness of a plate when it is by itself. Just so, it's impossible to estimate how skilled a worker is if they aren't measured against their teammates. Thus, the leader conducts an assessment of skills on their subordinates. The leader then rates their performance on a scale of 1 to 100 score system. This value denotes where an employee is in three levels of performance:

- Junior (from 1 to 30)

- Middle (30 to 70)

- Senior (from 70 to 100)

As we know, managers must ensure continuous growth, both in their employees and in their team overall. The manager must analyze the learning abilities of his or her staff and measure those against their complication of tasks. This is how you determine how effective an employee is. The basic principle of our company is self-improvement, and the firm's developmental plans do not allow stops or pauses in the growth process. If this does occur, the team will regress, impacting the whole organization.

The third column describes the level of employee loyalty. Here, the manager notes the Angle of the employee Vector of –90 to +90 degrees. They do this by analyzing the ways in which they and their staff best understand the philosophy of the company. At the same time, higher leadership will also evaluate the managers with respect to their positions. Even the CEO of the company calculates and compares the assessment of these managers. But all of these assessments take into account the potential human error in these assessments and the misunderstanding of low-level employees. By continually assessing this loyalty statistic, we're able to continually fine-tune the Vector Funnel and how its Angle is felt throughout the organization.

Loyality
60
30
30
-15
0
45
30
-5
0
75
90

The fourth column is Gravity. This shows how the employee attracts or rejects other members of the team. The manager scores on a 100-point system, judging the "magnetism" of employee, which is related to how each employee is able to change a colleague's thinking. Gravity is relatively constant, so take into account that these values may fluctuate based on the ebb and flow of employees and not how business is progressing. As a rule, it does not go beyond the boundaries of the existing regulations throughout the employees' work.

Gravity
21
48
91
67
20
14
15
13
53
67
25

Integration
21
38
80
67
20
25
15
20
53
67
40

This fifth column characterizes the level of employee Integration. With this data, the managers are able to evaluate how quickly the team communicates. Again, the scale is a 100-point score system. Often, Integration is closely related to Gravity, and the values of the two parameters are similar. Sometimes, there can be exceptions. In general, the level of this Integration is more flexible compared to Gravity. Certain tasks can spark genuine employee interest, and that can show a spike in the Integration data. This new task has become an Integration driver for the team members. It is worth noting that Integration, as well as Gravity, may not be recognized by a leader for a long time. Therefore, it is necessary to expose this column to a monthly review.

Flexibility	Rate of change
YES	55
YES	68
YES	30
NO	-
NO	-
YES	78
YES	10
YES	35
NO	-
YES	55
YES	64

The sixth and seventh columns relate to the employee's flexibility and rate of change. In order to gather this data, a manager must spend a few months of concentrated work preparing the team to face various problems in their day-to-day work. A good leader analyzes the results of an employee in these differing tasks in different areas. They then see if this pace makes them more productive or less productive in the workplace. Managers may express their opinions in this table in the form of a simple yes or no.

Based on this analysis, the manager can also document the speed of an employee's rate of change. The manager can rate this based on how quickly an employee moves from one task to another. This is a difficult value to change, and managers may spend untold man-hours in order to have a direct impact on their subordinate's workflow. In order to assess how long this process will take, a manager must evaluate the other values in the chart and make a final determination on their flexibility.

Our eighth column notes the level of chemistry. In this book, the concept of chemistry is treated as a relatively fleeting phenomenon between the new employee, the leader, and staff. This graph is required only for employees who are in the testing or probation period. This illustration will form a picture of future relationships on the team. Managers determine the chemistry by color. Employees who are linked by certain traits are marked by an individual color or shade.

After completing the data analysis, it is time for the manager to evaluate the Vector of employees. If the Vector Funnel is in the position from 0 to 90 degrees, there will be a clear minimum threshold of efficiency. If the manager finds an employee whose Vector does not conform to this particular Vector Funnel, they must be removed from the team or dismissed.

VECTOR OUSTS AN EMPLOYEE

Dismissal is far from a worst-case scenario. If a person is not suitable, it is necessary to part ways with such a disgruntled employee as quickly as possible. This will not only be able to save the company's time but also the time of the employee. Business should not have to agonize over these dead limbs. It is necessary to amputate and prevent further infection of the body. If this employee is indispensable and is the guardian of some knowledge without which the company cannot work, then you need to use your energy to bring this employee into your Funnel. And trust me, it won't be easy.

The task of the leader is to put their maximum effort into valuable employees and at least bring the others to a neutral state. An overall increase in the effectiveness of the team can be noticed immediately with the departure of a nonconforming employee. Because a team contains multitudes with varying Vectors, it is necessary that the manager use a certain approach in this termination or support. By going back to the Vector of the company, the manager is able to make the team part of the essential sphere of the organization.

Ideally, for a team to be successful, its members should not exceed ten employees. Thus, we form five teams of seven employees, with the total number of employees not exceeding thirty-five people. During the creation period, it is necessary for the leaders to follow the sequence of criteria outlined below:

1. **Selection of Gravitators:** First and foremost, the manager must select five employees with the most severe Gravity to ensure a stable leadership in the group. At the same time, total Gravity of all employees should not be above the Gravity of the main Gravitator (leader). The leader should be able to cope with his or her main task—gravitating Vectors in their direction and in the direction of the Vector of the company.

2. **Choice of Integrators:** If there are no Gravitators or their number is not large enough for Integration of a team, the leader selects the leading candidates through their integrative properties. Permanent working activities will allow the Integrator to successfully combine even a multi-Vectoral group under his or her leadership. If you have no Integrators, then the leader-

Gravitator needs an Integrator on the team to speed up the influence of the Gravitator on all others.

3. **Loyalty:** One of the most important factors of selecting a group leader is their loyalty. In order to guide the team, the leader must have a firm grasp of corporate philosophy, ethics, and history. However, the loyalty in the groups must be positive, or an Integrator can accelerate failure of the team.

4. **Efficiency and expertise:** Skills as well as the effectiveness of an employee are incredibly valuable when deciding the group leader. Assign an employee of the junior level to lead colleagues of a senior level, and you'll see it's not the best idea. Even in spite of the high level of Gravity and Integration, their efficiency can fall. Excessive loyalty of leader-beginners can frankly irritate professionals. To solve this issue, it is necessary to integrate a leader-mentor with a higher level of skills.

5. **Flexibility:** A candidate's ability to change is important also in group leaders. Today, employees might become the leader of the group by their ability to juggle multiple tasks. Tomorrow, they could be leaders of a unit. Readiness for dramatic change is one of the duties as well as key factors in leader selection.

6. **Chemistry**: It is important that the working unit is not only philosophically aligned but also aligned in their work ethic and rapport. A team should feel a level of camaraderie and support for each other that is hard to define or create.

After the formation of five teams in the current Funnel data, leaders should depict the Vector of each of the groups. By taking an organizational view of this data, higher management can strategize different management approaches for different business sectors. For example, if you can't form the team, then you should work with Gravitators individually. Create a business scheme where all the employees will connect with Gravitators. There should never be an employee separated from the business.

Higher management should give each group or team in their organization individual attention in order to encourage growth. In the course of the work, there will inevitably be a need for new employees. Urgency does not always mean who is in your hiring Funnel. It means right here and right now. As a rule, this urgent new hire might influence the staff's relation to the company Vector. In this case, you must add a colleague with twice as much Gravity as the other employees. The Vector of such an employee should be aimed as much as possible toward the Vector of the company.

It is important that the leader is a strong Gravitator and actively cooperates with other Gravitators. It is the manager who is responsible for introducing the team to corporate philosophy. Their process influences the general beliefs of the company. Interaction in the physical science describes the concept of a process where there is an exchange of particles between two bodies. During the formation of the team, the particles exchanged are the information that is transmitted every day during the course of communication. The more communication occurs between the colleagues, the more they are able to influence each other. In this situation, the value of Gravitators and Integrators is shown at the highest level. Gravitators create conditions for communication between individual employees, and Integrators speed up the process.

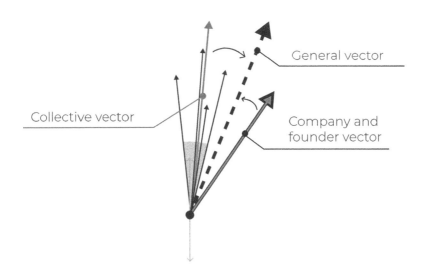

Over time, the total Gravitational Field becomes the most important factor in the formation of the collective Vector. At this point, it should have broken away from the founder's original Vector. The collective Vector is no longer influenced solely by the founder's Vector. The collective Vector now begins to affect the founder. Despite the fact that the Gravity of the founder is indisputably higher than that of the individual employees, the shared collective Vector may be stronger than the founder. This amassed Gravity will gradually pull the founder toward it, and during this process will change the Gravitational Field of the company and the very business philosophy of the company.

TIPS

1. Leaders begin to work on the formation of the collective Vector with a detailed chart that shows the current state of subordinates. Applicable documents should be updated at least once a month.

2. The manager must evaluate subordinates on a 100-point scale for the following parameters: **Skills, Loyalty, Gravity, Integration, Flexibility, Rate of Change, Chemistry.**

3. After analyzing the data, the manager determines the Funnel in accordance with the current Vector of the company. Employees' Vectors not aligned with the company's path should be removed or changed. For successful and productive teams, the number of employees should not exceed ten.

4. During the selection of the manager of a team, it is necessary to follow the sequence of criteria for the formation of the leaders of the group: **Gravity, Loyalty, Integration, Skills, Property and the Rate of Change, and Chemistry.**

5. After the formation of teams in the current Funnel, the leader should describe the Vector to each of the groups and think through the use of different methods for further changes.

6. The collective Vector, while instigated by the founder, can eventually influence and inform the founder's actions and goals.

CHAPTER 18

PROCESSES

At EnCata, we are deeply convinced that only the right people can build the right processes. But even carefully selected specialists with a correctly built Vector need support for solving nontrivial tasks based on modern business processes. We have tested and refined a number of solutions already implemented by major corporations. In certain areas, where managerial decisions were not enough, we have created our own approaches.

We've researched the best ways to manage from organizations across the world. It turns out that it's very difficult to find the precise solutions and techniques to run an international group of companies with an extensive business network. This chapter briefly highlights some of the processes and techniques that went into creating the Vector system. From agile to waterfall, we show how we merged our research of these myriad methodologies and processes into our single management philosophy.

PRODUCTION

The heart of the company is our manufacturing capability. Over the years, we have built processes to continuously improve the function of EnCata production lines. At the same time, we never hesitated to introduce well-known methodologies to our workshop to test them out. Every day, we made changes to the elements of employees' interactions with the work tools and products. We did this in an effort to change the market and the way consumers think about things. We make sure that our products are created on time and become a real breakthrough in their field.

WORKFLOW

If manufacturing is the heart of our company, the workflow of production is the steady beat that guides us along. As a basis for our workflow, we used the Toyota production system. The basic principles of Lean production philosophy, such as minimizing time losses and implementing quality control tools, fit perfectly into the EnCata philosophy. We found that the most important element in creating modern production is the process of streamlining. We realized that the FLOW of production keeps the whole company accountable.

FLOW is a special method of organizing work characterized by a number of specific features. These features are the following:

1. Separation of the general process of the product into separate components or operations

2. Consolidation of each operation for each and every workplace and machine; also, consolidating the specialization of the labor processes

3. Continuation of work at the same pace, but creating small incremental changes that gradually shift the flow of work

4. The location of operations and groups of similar equipment and capabilities during the period of change

Once all these things are in place, a production flow begins. Getting your production flow going from the start is key to growing your organization and its reach. Each phase of production brings new challenges and new features of workflow. These features include continuity and a strictly regulated rhythm of production, immediate transfer of raw materials between operations, synchronizing operations across the enterprise, a narrow specialization of jobs and machines, and application of specialized technological and transport equipment. The flow reduces the time to obtain the final product by about 80 percent.

After reading almost everything we could on Lean, we decided to meticulously follow the instructions of the experts. It's been about three years since we decided to establish these processes. In these years, we've cut ineffective parts of the system, resulting in huge savings and a more focused approach to our favorite parts of the business. With our experienced group of manufacturers, we created the first line of innovative projects through our flow system. This group would eventually go on to become senior members at EnCata.

Long before joining EnCata, our production manager led the assembly of window systems. At his disposal were several highly qualified specialists, each of whom assembled a part of the finished product. While he oversaw the full cycle of production operations, there were still gaps and hiccups outside of his purview. Even though his staff was highly competent, they spent a lot of time each day searching for specific tools necessary for production. Changes in the flow were needed to eliminate these halts in production.

After examining the situation, leadership built a new flow of production for these window systems. Separate work sites were created where manual labor could be done by untrained talent and products could be created simply with the use of a screwdriver. In order to cut down on the time spent searching for a specific tool, a screwdriver was located right next to every employee's workplace. After implementing each of these changes, leadership looked again at the flow of the whole system. The bottlenecking initially caused by overexperienced staff and lack of centralized locations for production and tools disappeared. Additionally, the cost of maintaining workers markedly decreased.

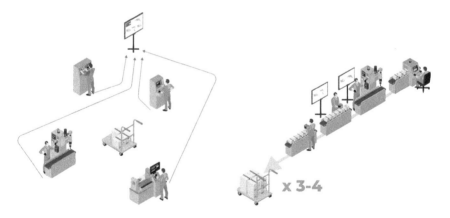

Based on the experience of our product manager, we created a similar system for workflow but adapted it to the unique needs and desires of EnCata. At the time, we wanted to build a stream for a single product and not mass production like the window systems. At EnCata, we've created a system of workstations that handle a singular task for production. Each workstation is stocked with the equipment designed for its specific operation. In order to keep production moving, our specialists must not only be highly talented but flexible enough to move between workstations whenever necessary. That being said, we try to keep the movement between workstations to a minimum, for simplicity's sake. We took many elements from Lean production and complemented the corporate philosophy with the main points of the work of Collins, Adizes, and Altshuller (TRIZ).

The main objective of the Lean manufacturing concept is to strive to eliminate all types of losses. These losses could be defined as those actions that consume resources but do not create value. Within the system, all actions are divided into those that bring and do not bring the final value of the product to the consumer. So the goal of Lean at EnCata is to arrange production in such a way that there are no expectations and downtime in the process. One of the elements introduced in our production is the 5S board.

5S BOARDS

5S is a system for organizing and rationalizing jobs. We simplified our job system so that it reflects one of the following five qualities:

1. Sorting
2. Maintaining order
3. Keeping clean
4. Standardizing
5. Improving

The board is the primary element of our flow system. It helps employees understand not only the flow of production throughout the system but also where key elements need to be placed in order for the system to work properly. A diagram on the board indicates where each instrument should be placed. This helps employees instantly determine where a tool belongs and where to return it after it is used.

After the introduction of the board, we constantly began to tweak it and adapt it, tailoring it to fit the actual operations of our production system. We wanted to make sure that our employees had maximum control over their workstations and equipment. In our tinkering, we came to the conclusion that in order to achieve this, the use of a neural network was necessary. This is how the idea of the world's first 5S whiteboard based on machine learning algorithms came up.

A neural network is a mathematical model for creating machines with artificial intelligence. These machines mimic the human brain using algorithms that help them learn and advance their knowledge of the task they are designed to do. Today, they are already used in many areas of human activity. So we decided to use them to improve our 5S board and in turn our production.

On each board, we marked a special area to designate where each instrument should go. These markings help the network determine which tool is not in place and where to place it. In addition, we added special strips at the perimeter of the board. If the camera cannot see the strip, it cannot capture the board. This sometimes happens if a person blocks the camera's view. When the camera sees the strips again, the system resumes its operations.

Every second, the camera takes a shot of the board. That image is then processed through the neural network, which determines the level of compliance and order of the board. The system also detects the accuracy of the placement of tools. If a tool is misplaced in a spot on the board, the system alerts us. The system also allows us to better understand when the tools are being used and how. Finally, if an unauthorized user gains access to the tools and tries to use them, the system immediately alerts management.

One improvement we chose to make in EnCata's production system was the introduction of the "Andon button." We have ours located directly on the rack of the system where the 5S

board is located. The Andon button is a device for visual control of the production area. It warns workers about defects, malfunctions, or other problems by using coordinated signals of lights and sound. At EnCata, the Andon button has a siren at the top. In the event of an unsolvable task, the employee presses the button, the siren lights up, and the engineer of a project is obliged to go to the worker and find out the cause of the problem. At the same time, we stop the line for the production of the device exactly until the problem is resolved.

To visualize the state of the workflow and the availability of necessary materials, we use Kanban carts, which move from workstation to workstation. Kanban is a signal for action, a tool for managing flows and production of products in the "pull" system adopted by Toyota. We have completely adopted this system, and thanks to the visual color display of the work being performed and the availability of materials, we reduced the communication time between specialists from different production sites.

Moreover, each employee of the EnCata workshop is required to note their working hours and individual processes in the internal CRM system. Our CRM system was developed in house at EnCata Soft. At production, its simplified version is used with the ability to mark the time and get basic information on projects and tasks. This was done to reduce the billable time of specialists in the workshop and accurately assess the information that does not directly affect the process or the quality of the work performed.

Finally, each machine, each section, and each tool are marked with a QR code. The employee starts by scanning the code to get access to the project. In the process, they scan the material used to make the part. This allows not only a reduction in the time to communicate with other employees to  clarify operations, but also an analysis of all statistics on the expenditure of time and materials. The system notes the time, materials, and capacities spent by the employee and keeps records in the internal CRM—EnCata Internal. This system will be available for purchase soon.

INNOVATIVE OPENSPACE SYSTEM

While this all seems very regimented, it actually allows for much more freedom for the employee. Every EnCata office is designed to take advantage of open floor plans and innovative workstations. Each employee has free access to boards signaling the stages of a project and reminding employees responsible for completing the development phase on time.

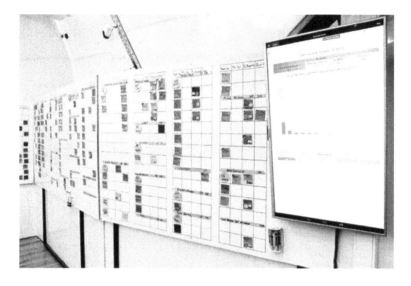

A project leader can track the "movement" of a project online, thanks to the implemented statistical system, which creates infographics based on the main data. These infographics are then displayed on screens behind the workplace of department heads and the CEO of the company.

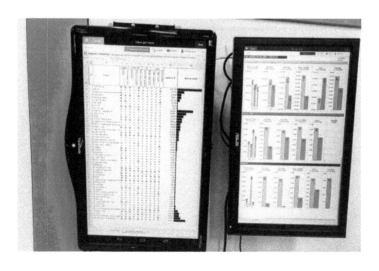

Within the EnCata production system, the CEO is endowed with special powers. Thanks to the integration of CRM systems, digital Kanban boards, and the availability of data, online company management is carried out with one click. Each employee receives inquiries with the possibility of monosyllabic answers. They note the hours spent on a certain activity. All this data makes it possible for the CEO or leader to spend only one or two hours monitoring the company's indicators directly from their smart mobile device.

During work hours, we pay special attention to our employees' desktops. For them, this is the place where they spend about a third of their lives. Their working space should not only be as comfortable as possible but also have the flexibility to adapt to the employee's current project. So the workstation of any employee is mobile. Tables of our own production are equipped with wheels that can change direction. This allows leaders to collect teams for projects within a few minutes.

Thanks to our open floor plan and our flexible workstations, our employees can converge and disperse based on the needs of the production flow. A project team can have from two to several dozen people. Making sure that all employees are present at these connected workstations ensures that work is completed in the shortest amount of time. Such mobile teams allow the company to physically manage the volume of work for each of the projects and rationally distribute human potential in a limited space. Additionally, we practice maximum transparency in the visual organization of the workplace. We do not have closed cabinets and racks. If the item is not in its place, then this will become a clear signal for the employee to take action.

To achieve control over the stages of product development, we structure these mobile teams around "posts." These "posts" are screens that display the stage and name of the project currently being worked on. The screen also displays the serial number of the project so employees can align to specific stages of these high-tech projects. Individual employees know to congregate around a certain "post" based on their daily workload and current project obligations.

To assess the stages of these projects, we use the methodology of technology readiness levels developed by NASA. These techniques were developed to classify the readiness for application of various technologies created and commercialized by scientists and engineers. Each qualitative advancement toward the creation of a commercial product or technology underlying the product is called **TRL** (technology readiness level).

At EnCata, we solve our tough production problems with the use of the TRIZ system. Developed by a Soviet inventor and scientist, this methodology helps us come up with inventive problem-solving techniques to tackle big challenges. To organize office work, we use the classic team management methodologies. For team management at EnCata, we dive deep into the luscious taste of waterfall with agile. We then season our style with Toyota's original Lean philosophy.

While we have these methodologies in place, we never discourage our employees from creating their own best practices. In fact, we encourage our staff to innovate within their own software. They do so by taking advantage of our digital Kanban cards and using their own CRM system—EnCata Internal.

SOFTWARE

For years, EnCata used third-party CRMs to set, manage, and control workloads. We began to realize, however, that these systems had their own shortcomings and malfunctions that we had to spend time eliminating or maneuvering around. The vast majority of these systems had such problems. That's when we decided to create our own CRM system that would run the way we wanted it to. It took a year to create, but we completed it and deployed it across the organization.

Today, EnCata Internal is being improved by a separate division of the company—EnCata Soft. This team has experience in these tailor-made software systems. They already use one for their

accounting and labor reports. Within this program, employees must pass a test of three questions that relate to company standards. If the employee passes every test within a month, they are entitled to a bonus. This is how we track our employees' knowledge and ensure they are aligned to the company's.

These standard tests are placed in a separate part of the system, where managers can create and approve them for employees. Based on their own projects, they can also create tests unique to their team. On the main screen of the system, the employee is daily shown the work tasks and terms for them, as well as the standards necessary for reading and testing. In addition,

each member of the EnCata team can offer an improvement related to absolutely any area of the company's activity. From a modification to the workplace, a change in processes, or even the purchase of another brand of milk for the coffee machine, we want our employees to help us create a better EnCata together. If a proposal is approved by the unit heads, the employee is awarded a prize.

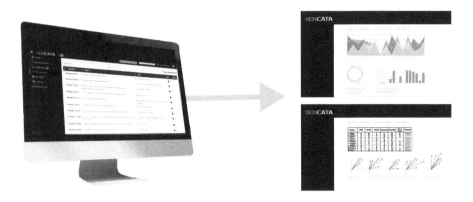

We also paid special attention to the Vector system in EnCata Internal. An additional block implements software for department heads and the CEO of the company, where the manager enters data for each subordinate and as a result receives a clearly constructed Vector of an employee and recommendations on team building. The leader also receives information on the dynamics of the Vector field. They can see data for each employee, for the unit, and for the company as a whole.

Today, we are ready to share our software with the world. Each section of EnCata has embarked on its own path of innovation in creating its software. We sincerely believe that our pioneering software will become a quick tool for managing any business. Customers that choose to incorporate our software will reap the most valuable resource—time. They can then use it to create the most important thing for their organization—a corporate philosophy. Additionally, you can get this software to maintain your own business via the Vector system at www.kondrashov.biz.

CHAPTER 19

ENCATA AND BEYOND

If, ten years ago, someone told me that I would be managing my own technology park, I would not have been surprised. About a decade ago, I figured out how to refill a printer cartridge more efficiently than anyone else did in my country. Five years ago, I created an international innovative business with representation in six countries. A year ago, the company became one of the first private technology parks in Eastern Europe. Today, you read my book in whatever country and whatever language it has reached you in.

Yes, you understood correctly—in these chapters there will be no false modesty and lengthy statements. If you want to experience our sweet slogans and branded language of our marketers, then I invite you to read the entire twelve-page list of our services on our EnCata site. This book contains only real achievements and scenarios based on corporate philosophy.

A few years ago, we had founded a company that successfully produced air purification equipment. Despite excellent profitability, we did not slow down, and we realized our engineering potential in a completely new industry. This was all happening at the beginning of an era of the global start-up insanity movement. Suddenly, Californians in T-shirts and hoodies were not the only ones who could roll out idea after idea. From across North America, Eastern and Western Europe, and even Southeast Asia, start-ups fired up and fell apart right before our collective eyes. Young talent was crafting incredible new projects virtually every day. True, many of these fledgling entrepreneurs had no idea how to implement their rollout strategies, but certainly we at EnCata were and are ready! We wanted to help these great ideas find a home and flourish.

ENCATA THE CATALYST

EnCata is a catalyst for the implementation of new ideas and technologies from many countries. We're bringing to life—and trying to bring to market—what only yesterday seemed like the fairy tales of science fiction writers. What first started as EnCata outsourcing its engineering expertise has become a kind of mentorship program for these small start-ups. We've gradually connected these start-ups to additional resources for training in management, marketing, and other business processes. Today, EnCata is a full-fledged partner and mentor in the global start-up movement. Our position in Eastern Europe gives us a great advantage to find new opportunities from companies who have no access to capital markets.

We're training and trying to bring projects from Belarus and other countries to the global market by entering the markets via Eastern Europe. Today, we're also gaining a foothold in countries from the Middle East, Western Europe, and North America. In addition, we are beginning to work out ways to enter the countries of Southeast Asia and Oceania. We are also opening up our services not only to small projects and promising start-ups but also to large businesses.

Even multinational corporations can turn to EnCata to implement almost any technological spin-off we've had a hand in. Such clients are primarily interested in the confidentiality of development. When it comes to the data of our partners, the information is unique, closed, and maximally protected. Only direct customers receive limited access to the company's protected information because we understand intellectual theft and piracy. This chapter gives you a sampling of some of our projects. Each of the projects listed below gave their personal permission to post the details of their products in this book.

Over the years of engineering work, we have developed several important ethical principles in dealing with customers. We fundamentally refuse projects related to weapons and everything that can directly or indirectly harm a person or any other living creature. We actively support projects related to global challenges and allowing us to solve the fundamental problems of humanity: diseases, hunger, overpopulation, and natural disasters.

(All of the projects that follow are in different stages of development.)

MEDICAL PROJECTS

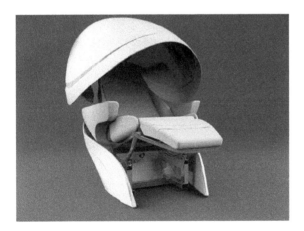

One of the first EnCata products in the medical sector was the Reyou Capsule—a pod for sleep. The Reyou Capsule is the latest achievement in the unlimited and still unexplored area of human sleep. It is impossible to overestimate the influence of sleep on physiological and mental health. This company is creating cutting-edge technology that will affect how we all sleep in the future. Issues such a sleep deprivation, sleep apnea, and other rest ailments are at the forefront of their work. This relatively inexpensive device is designed to significantly reduce stress of individuals, no matter what their relation to sleep might be. The capsule scans all vital signs and creates a carefully selected atmosphere using sounds and lighting solutions. Recovering lost sleep within twenty to forty minutes allows the sufferer to get a good night's sleep. This capsule allows people to return to their work well rested and ready to go. This product can be put virtually anywhere—at the airport or in your office. It organically fits into any interior.

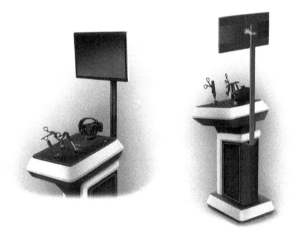

Surgery is a stress not only for the patient's body but also on the surgeon's mind. In order to prepare a surgeon for this experience, we have developed an advanced simulator for the most modern methods of surgery. Based on virtual reality technology, MedVR gives a surgeon the most realistic and advanced simulation—the closest to the real surgery as possible. Trained specialists can be inserted into any type of laparoscopic surgery. We hope soon to use MedVR in the special training for neurosurgeons.

ARIADNA is a project that allows for the medical specialist to combine and visualize computed tomography, MRI, and x-ray data using mixed reality technologies. Augmented and 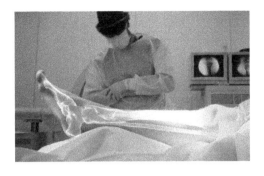 virtual reality represent the studied patient data as a whole and reduce the time required for planning the operation. Moreover, the patient receives less radiation during the examination due to the reduction in the number of procedures.

The main goal of this software is recognizing and translating sign language. The program removes the communication barrier for patients with hearing or speech impairment. The system understands gestures in real time and works through a webcam or smartphone. The software allows people with disabilities to view video content without a need for a sign language translation.

EnCata has made every effort to change the approach to diagnosing diseases through Hippocrates—our machine learning diagnosis system. Our machine learning technology has created a neural network that tracks the current state of the body systems and shows changes based on a comparative analysis of previous data with maximum accuracy. The device is destined to become a breakthrough in the diagnosis and prevention of diseases due to its small size, amazing accuracy, and relatively affordable price.

AEROSPACE

The LRET Antenna is able to issue a high-quality signal over a long distance, helping advance communication in the era of globalization. The antenna is a digital system that allows you to transmit a signal through any physical objects. Design features in the LRET Antenna provide the ability to reduce the size of the transmission device by ten times. The frequency ranges from 30 Hz to 60 kHz, which allows the signal to cover more than 3,700 miles. Innovation allows the user to create geolocation systems with an accuracy of fifteen inches and minimal coverage costs. The ramifications of this product would further help build emerging smart cities.

CONSUMER PRODUCTS

SmartCup is an innovative product that transforms a familiar mug into a smart device. The SmartCup makes hot beverages using sophisticated methods, brewing different varieties of tea and coffee. In addition, the SmartCup is able to maintain the temperature of whatever is inside it, including beverages, soup, and even baby food. The functionality of the device allows users to enjoy their favorite drinks at a convenient time. And it is completely mobile ready, allowing users to enjoy their SmartCup with one click.

Smart Cork is a technological replacement of the cork for alcoholic drinks in modern drinking establishments. The device monitors the amount of fluid consumed, signals the need for replenishment, and also provides control over the actions of bartenders in the process of working activity. The Smart Cork consistently moderates the liquid in the bottle to ensure flavor and safety of consumption. This is transmitted directly to the product owner through a mobile application. It can also be integrated into inventory systems, allowing the user to account for customer demands. The Smart Cork can also be used for counterfeit prevention and theft. Finally, the system can determine the dosage of certain drugs, allowing it to be used in the medical field as well.

AirZen is a personalized desktop air purifier with integrated climate control. The device controls humidity, temperature, ionization level, CO_2 level, and even air aroma. It also kills viruses and creates a secure area near the workspace. Creating an individual comfortable microclimate is achieved through personal settings via a mobile application.

AGRICULTURAL PROJECTS

EnCata has helped develop a special innovative plant nutrient environment known as Ionite Soil. This product ensures effective plant growth by providing seedlings with a complete list of chemicals that help plants develop. Crops in this system have unique abilities. Their growth is practically unlimited by physical obstacles. They can grow anywhere, including walls, ceilings, and other surfaces.

CONSTRUCTION PROJECTS

Cuby House is not a start-up. It's not just another project we've worked on at EnCata. This is a global transformation of the real estate market. Robotic stations operating completely offline in the very near future will erect buildings directly on the construction site. Construction times will be reduced by three times. The costs are half of current or previous methodologies. The Cuby project integrates its own IoT devices into the assembly points of walls, floors, and ceilings. The system will assume accommodation by subscription instead of the usual mortgages and rents.

SERVICES PROJECTS

THE PSYCHO reimagines the VR gaming industry. A full-fledged technological suit allows the player to become fully immersed in the virtual world. Motion sensors, oculus virtual reality glasses, and a hardware backpack offer an incredible gaming experience to even the most sophisticated gamers.

Aerocapsule is a secluded cabin for people to find solitude in travel stations—airports, train stations, and ports. It may also be used for coworking. The capsule provides high noise cancellation and allows the user to escape from the hustle and bustle of the trip and continue to work online in a quiet environment. The capsule is equipped with modern ventilation, lighting systems, Wi-Fi modules, and comfortable chairs. The external area of the capsule serves as a space for advertising placement—installing a video screen outside is one of the options of the model.

THE FINANCIAL SECTOR

Vouchers is a system for controlling the targeted distribution of funds based on blockchain technology. Quorum technology is the basis for this project that is actively used in the banking sector. It allows you to track transactions and spending with utmost transparency. The main objective of the project is the effective fight against corruption at each stage of the movement of capital.

NEW MATERIALS

The Rubber Recycling project solves the problem of tire recycling through a special approach to the devulcanization method. Using environmentally friendly technology, we have developed a mixture of devulcanized rubber that is easier to break down and recycle. We have shown the profitability and feasibility of devulcanized rubber use in a wide range of other products such as gas masks and used tires.

INFRASTRUCTURE DEVELOPMENT PROJECTS

Classical hackerspaces located in the world's hardware capitals have never been structured organizations. As a rule, their creators and managers are as far from real production as possible. At EnCata, we've gone against this notion and incorporated our hackerspace directly into our production line. For the first time in Minsk, we created a creative full-fledged hackerspace where engineers and students can use the most modern equipment and simple CNC machines for research and prototyping.

The MakeIT Center allows start-ups to get their product ready for rollout as quickly as possible. Users can rent a machine to start work on their project. If they don't have the skills necessary to operate this machine, they can rent a technician who can become a part of their innovative start-up. We started this space with a Cold War bunker and half a million dollars of investment, knowing full well we'd likely never see that money again. We have overcome long odds on our path

to world markets. This project feeds the engineering gene pool and enables conditions for genetic development and will expand over time. It may take decades, but this innovation has the potential to change populated regions' ideas of prospective hardware projects.

This list is in no way complete. At EnCata, we're constantly tinkering and toying with countless new ideas until we hit on one that breathes new life into our company and the world. We have even created a MakeIT school for beginners to learn more about technology. Do you have an idea that you want to work on? EnCata looks forward to hearing from you.

Ten years ago, we refilled cartridges and created toys connected to the internet. Now, we seek to change the appearance of the world around us. But we are still ready for challenges and discoveries.

Everyone, be it a corporation, start-up, or job seeker, can become part of our technological progress. Everyone can become a part of EnCata. You know how to find me. My name is Oleg Kondrashov. I am "the man from Minsk."

BEYOND WORK—THE VECTOR IN OUR LIVES

ROD ROBERTSON

As an American and Oleg's coauthor, I believe that after reading the prior chapters, the reader cannot refute the logic in using the Vector in the workplace. The premises of this philosophy allow for the cultivation of an efficient and successful business. But we are not just work machines! We must all maintain our balance of work, love, and play. We all know those workaholics driven to exhaustion and ill health, whose understanding of life is driven by money making, fame, and glory. These human business machines suffer untold pain and misery as they sacrifice all aspects of their life in pursuit of business success.

If this book has awakened you to the efficiencies of the Vector at work, why not apply these same dynamics to all facets of your life? Creating a balance of home life, friends, exercise, and other pursuits will make for a much happier experience in our lives. *Stress* is the great killer. The whole premise of the Vector is to eliminate stress and become more efficient in the workplace. Harmony with fellow employees creates great workflow but also eases tension and anxiety.

THE HOME FRONT

Our spouses, companions, and significant others impact our lives in various ways, but they all have one thing in common. In order to have a good relationship with them, we must all be in the same groove—the same Vector. If there are little monsters underfoot, they, too, can be steered by the Vector. We all try, consciously or subconsciously, to bring harmony and efficiency to our home. To be aware of the power of the Vector, we can evaluate our relationships at home and throughout our extended family. The Vector allows us to bring order from chaos. You don't have to go deep into the Vector. No need to make charts for your family tree! But you can architect a better and healthier life program for your loved ones.

Whether you are a parent in charge of a family or a single person living alone, we can all benefit from this scientific approach to our lives. And why not? This certainly is the time and age to do it. The internet has enabled the Vector to get to work in thousands of ways by seeking out harmony and flow in all facets of our lives.

THE VECTOR IN ROD'S LIFE

Becoming friends with Oleg and digging deep into his world has been a startling experience for me. To a certain extent, I have been practicing in my own orderly mental system an informal Vector program. But my life has been full of clutter. Hundreds of new and old relationships have brought chaos to me and have sucked valuable resources out of my life. These relationships have veered me into channels that were not accretive to my life. In addition, my existence has been dominated by work, which has brought even more chaos and stress. The quest to balance home, work, friendship, and personal wellness is a difficult task, maybe even an impossible one. But by understanding who we are and organizing our life through the Vector system, we can find that elusive balance.

I will use the Human Vector to guide my activities at work. This will waterfall into other areas so that I may squeeze in as much fulfillment as possible. I will be able to visit more places and use my financial resources more wisely, but most importantly, I will be able to spend my life with people of like mind and purpose.

OLEG KONDRASHOV

So, you've read our book cover to cover. Along the way you learned something new about Eastern Europe and how business works here. You got to know your employees again thanks to our Vector theory. You also now understand what projects EnCata has been preparing for mass production and entering the global market.

By the time this book is published, our world will have changed beyond recognition. As we all too painfully know, in early 2020, the entire world economy "went into quarantine" due to the pandemic. At the time of this writing, the virus's toll is accelerating, and there is no cure in sight, so if you are reading this text, I hurry to congratulate you: you are alive! This is an achievement in and of itself. In case you managed to save your business and adapt to new conditions at work, you can safely look forward to new heights, because the horizon, driven by technology, is clearer than ever.

Despite all the sad upheavals that we have experienced, the pandemic allowed us to prove the effectiveness of Vector theory even as we all sought a new equilibrium. In perfect sailing conditions, a ship under a captain's clear instructions with a crew ready to work seemed unsinkable in conditions of calm seas. Now, however, the days of smooth sailing are long gone.

In today's new reality, cohesive teams ready for any turn of the rudder under the sensitive guidance of a flexible captain are breaking through wave after wave of the new economic reality. The crew's strength was enough to withstand the storm; their vision helped to find the way where others saw the approaching rocks only too late. The captain for this new age needs the courage to take a number of nonstandard decisions, creating around him the halo of a person leading through the most difficult obstacles. If you are still trying to swim out of the whirlpool of a global catastrophe, then perhaps this book is exactly the lifeline that you need now. The experience of transformation in the new environment is unlikely to be avoidable for a businessman of any level. And now we're going to talk about ours.

From the very beginning of the pandemic, we realized that we would have to shelve our high-tech projects and prepare simple and effective solutions based on the technologies available here and now. That's what happened: about 80 percent of our customers have curtailed their prepandemic projects, driven by the preservation of their businesses as we collectively swallowed our pride to adapt to our new job functions. In our world, our jobs have turned into a grueling twenty-hour daily marathon—but this too shall pass. The prize was the future of the company, the future of each of the employees.

At EnCata and our subsidiaries, we quickly pivoted to products that today allow thousands of people around the world to be at work without fear by developing a new high-end antiviral mask.

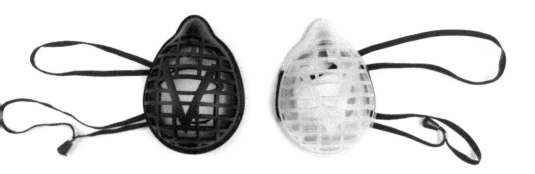

Our revolutionary mask features unique replaceable bioactive filters, which destroy bacteria and can hold the virus at bay for forty hours of uninterrupted work. This technological breakthrough gave us the impetus to develop the company in a most unexpected direction.

Our Vizard mask holder

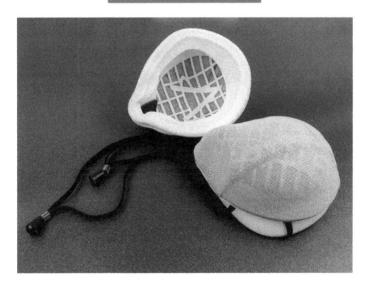

We have joined the global race to expand our range of personal protective equipment.

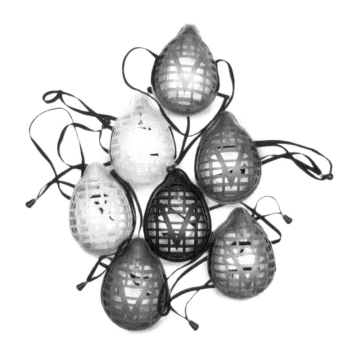

Thus, the Vizard mask holder is equipped with three different types of filters for different conditions and requirements for air purification. Moreover, the set now includes a shield that additionally protects the face even in crowded places. This solution is not an innovation, nor does it bring profit to the company. For us, it is the minimum measure of support for the world citizenry in this difficult situation.

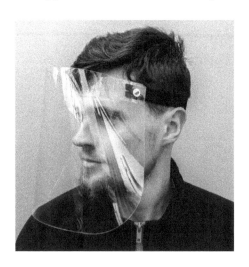

We have also rapidly pivoted to develop a product called G|0 Gate. The reference to patient zero in the name itself indicates that the product is designed to detect infected people in crowded areas with the slightest change in temperature and the first symptoms of COVID-19.

Innovations used in the Gate kit solve the problem of decontamination. Visitors find themselves in an ion air stream that destroys bacteria and viruses on the body and clothing. Also, the device's technologies allow it to determine if the user's sense of smell is working. During the medical check, G|0 Gate sprays one of several sharp smells and detects dangerous  viruses based on the buttons pressed by the user on a special module.

We tried to adapt the rest of the products as much as possible to the current situation. The Fir airframe building became a rapidly deployable field hospital, while our other capacities were immediately focused on the development of the internal arrangement of similar structures. We realized that some of our products would remain in the "old world" and reoriented the company as quickly as needed to survive.

The process of transformation did not just take place in our products. We were able to make every decision immediately thanks to our teamwork and belief in the company's Vector.

I will not deny the fact that we have resorted to cost optimization, including the payroll. We had to temporarily limit the growth of salaries, and a portion of the payroll decreased by 10–20 percent. In this crisis situation, the vast majority of our employees understood even unpopular measures. Everyone understands that every effort must be made to keep the ship afloat in this new environment.

Our team began to work more and more, not stopping on weekends and holidays. I would need another book to describe my gratitude to my people for being more united than ever and for adapting to these new conditions in just one month. We have created and put into mass production products that would normally take over a year of hard work. Precise execution of orders, transparent feedback, and dedication have done their job. Our team took on the new challenge with a revived spirit that began to show the motivation of each employee. We proved to be more maneuverable than other ships thanks to the advantages of the Vector system.

It's obvious that EnCata is a niche international player in the large scheme of things, with limited resource funds. But at the same time, in our opinion EnCata is a single command Vector, which still brings together the best engineering minds of Belarus. At this difficult time, we as managers do not cast away from our employees—when the postcrisis indicators are tallied, everyone will be compensated for their financial losses. Even in case of an inevitable breakup with a part of the team, we will help our wards to find work regardless of the situation on the labor market.

During the crisis, we are now forced to recruit more unskilled workers to work at simple production sites. We launched twenty-four-hour work in three shifts and gave an opportunity to improve financial situations to one of the most vulnerable segments of society: disabled people and students. They are new to our team, but these new employees have quickly changed their Vectors in becoming loyal to the strong common Vector of the company. Some of EnCata's employees have rapidly become shift supervisors for the new employees, exhibiting their previously hidden organizational and leadership skills.

Everyone feels not just like a screw in the system but rather like a driving element. We all believe we can change the process alone if necessary. I myself sometimes work in our workshop; this is how I relax from the grinding around-the-clock routine. New recruits may have seen for the first time that they are treated with due respect and appreciation for their work. For many new employees during this pandemic, they unexpectedly came out much faster, beginning to generate ideas themselves and implement them. The common Vector not only opened up individual traits, but also turned the team into a single fast-moving machine plowing through barriers. The ingenuity of our engineers working with a common Vector and turning an idea into reality in days is attributed to the company Vector. You can't buy this camaraderie and team play. This team commitment and natural ingenuity are priceless.

We have faced excessive bureaucracy, like many organizations around the world. However, American and European companies are often stymied by regulations, which may delay things several years— unacceptable in a pandemic. Life-altering businesses need to become nimbler, or we will pay the consequences—if not this time, then next time. Today, R&D centers must deliver new products within weeks, and testing laboratories must be open to inspect such products as soon as possible.

The dark underbelly of this rushed worldwide innovation of much-needed technologies is the proliferation of dark forces siphoning the good work of the majority. Unfortunately, it is also our daily duty to combat such defiant manifestations of human nature. However, despite all these misfortunes, we all must remain a force that does not put profit above humanity.

ABOUT THE AUTHORS

OLEG KONDRASHOV
"THE MAN FROM MINSK"

Oleg is a tech entrepreneur in Europe who has developed a unique scientific approach to bringing his technology companies to market. A physicist, Oleg is uniquely qualified as a scientist to have developed a proven system of developing start-ups and technology that increases their value in a nine-step process.

Oleg, at age thirty-five, is the CEO of his organization, which has a portfolio of fifty companies at various stages of development. His firm (www.encata.net) is an incubator with over two hundred employees, of which the majority are engineers and software programmers. They work with fledgling European companies that have outstanding technology that needs to be deployed into the global marketplace.

Oleg and his partners are viewed as a leading business development organization in Belarus. Their team is optimally located to be a beneficiary of the vast talent pool of programmers, engineers, and inventors of Eastern Europe. His operations have a growing Funnel for entrepreneurs who have no experience in taking their companies to market. Oleg and his team are expanding his operations into the

United States as his portfolio of tech companies seek strategic partners, additional funding, and robust customer bases.

His team has built an assembly line of first-class companies from multiple industries that have proven themselves capable of global tier-one products.

ROD ROBERTSON

Rod is an international entrepreneur who has done business in over fifteen countries and has spent a lifetime developing small-to-medium-sized businesses and taking them to market worldwide. As a former three-time business owner and current owner of a boutique international investment bank (www.briggscapital.com) based in Boston, Rod has surfed for decades with entrepreneurs in their quest to monetize their holdings.

Rod, as managing partner of Briggs Capital for twenty years, has tremendous experience in bringing growing international firms to the US marketplace. He and his team bring stateside talent to companies as they look to deploy their technology and products to the US marketplace. Rod and his associates are adept at valuating enterprises, raising funds for growth, and leading companies to lucrative exits.

Rod has authored a well-received book, *Winning at Entrepreneurship,* and is a public and motivational speaker on multiple platforms. Rod is a frequent past and current guest lecturer at the Harvard Business School and other topflight MBA schools around the world and is a contributor to multiple media outlets, ranging from television to podcasts to major print outlets. Rod serves on multiple boards of higher education, banks, and private growth companies.

ACKNOWLEDGMENTS

FROM OLEG:

Gratitude to my wife, Tatiana; my mother; my partners, Sergey Tkachenko and Dr. Peter Dudin; and all the employees who work or have worked with me. You all helped me to realize what I wrote above. Thank you.

Special thanks for help in writing this book to Alex Kurbatov. Also gratitude to Michael Verenov for help in translation.

FROM ROD:

A tip of our hat to Josh, our editor, and to Rachel, our Advantage project manager, who worked endless hours to bridge the language and cultural gaps that arise with such a cross-cultural undertaking!

DEFINITIONS AND TERMINOLOGY

THE VECTOR:
A systematic and scientific approach of management to assess, evaluate, and maximize employee performance.

GRAVITY:
The ability to attract other employees and change their Vector Angle.

VECTOR LENGTH:
The professionalism of an employee.

THE ANGLE:
Employees' loyalty to the organization and relationship to the Vector.

MATHLETE:
An individual with excellent mathematics skills.

THE GRAVITATOR:
An individual who is able to change Angles of employees by force of personality.

KPI:

Key performance indicator.

TRL:

Technology readiness level (developed by NASA).

INTEGRATION:

The movement and formation of Vectors; an incentive for growth.

INTEGRATOR:

A person who accelerates interactions between people in a company.

MASS EFFECT:

The process of mass interdependent chain changes in the Angles. Mass movement of employees can dilute or slow growth of the company Vector.

GRAVITATIONAL FIELDS:

Numbers of magnets (created by a company's ecosystem) that change Vectors of its employees.

FUNNEL OF VECTORS:

Acceptable deviation of employees from the company Vector.

DISINTEGRATOR:

A person who slows down or stops interaction between people in a company.

Printed in the USA
CPSIA information can be obtained
at www.ICGtesting.com
JSHW072028140824
68134JS00044B/3823